The New Dimension
of the Soul

THE NEW DIMENSION
OF THE SOUL

Chapel Addresses by
RICHARD KRONER

Foreword by
HENRY PITNEY VAN DUSEN

Edited by
JOHN E. SKINNER

Fortress Press   Philadelphia

To

Reinhold Niebuhr

in gratitude

FOREWORD

It is a privilege as well as a pleasure to commend this volume to the widest possible reading public.

For over a decade Dr. Richard Kroner and I were colleagues on the Faculty of Union Theological Seminary, New York. During all those years when these sermons were being preached in the James Memorial Chapel of the Seminary, because of conflicting Sunday appointments elsewhere I do not think I ever had the opportunity to hear my honored friend and associate in the pulpit. Therefore, this admirable collection speaks to me with almost the same freshness which it will have for those who have known Dr. Kroner only by reputation or through his writings or perhaps not known him at all.

One of the striking facts in the world of religion in our day is the great influence exerted through their preaching by men who are primarily theologians, and the even wider helpfulness of their sermons when published. To mention only three, all theological co-workers and intimate comrades of Richard Kroner, one thinks at once of the volumes of sermons by Reinhold Niebuhr, Paul Tillich, and David E. Roberts. The large and continuing demand for their preaching-in-print bears eloquent testimony to the presence of a very considerable public, outside as well as within formal church membership, who welcome and are prepared to feed upon solid meat of sermonic theology.

To the steadily lengthening shelf of such books is now added this anthology from the mind and spirit and voice of one of the noblest Christians whom any of us has known. Like Paul Tillich, Richard Kroner was an unintended benefaction to the United States and its churches from Hitler's tyranny. Exiled from his beloved fatherland, to which he is still knit by ties of affection and loyalty, Dr. Kroner first found refuge in Scotland at the University of St. Andrews, where he was honored with appointment to the most distinguished lectureship in religion in the English-speaking world; his Gifford Lectures were published under the title *The Primacy of Faith.*

In 1942, Dr. Kroner crossed to the United States to join the Union Seminary teaching staff, first as lecturer and then as adjunct professor. He at once took his place with the quiet dignity and insistent modesty which are measures of his deep Christian character as a teacher of profound learning, penetrating perceptiveness, and contagious ardor, universally valued and beloved by his students. They will join his theological colleagues and, it is to be hoped, a very much more numerous company of grateful readers in welcoming these testimonies of personal faith, complementing the substantial works in theology with which their author has already enriched Christian thought in our day.

HENRY PITNEY VAN DUSEN
President Emeritus
Union Theological Seminary

Sorrento, Maine
September, 1963

EDITOR'S PREFACE

Richard Kroner has pursued two careers. He distinguished himself as one of the outstanding philosophers in pre-Hitler Germany. His reputation as an authority on German Idealism, his involvement in many learned societies in Europe, his editorship of the international journal of culture, *Logos,* and the professorships he held at the Universities of Freiburg, Dresden, and Kiel, established him as one of the important thinkers and scholars of the world. But, like so many of Germany's creative sons, he was by the barbarism of the Nazi movement forced into exile from his native land.

Kroner's second career began in England and achieved its greatest acclaim in the United States. At Union Theological Seminary in New York, the refugee philosopher concentrated upon the relation of philosophy to the Christian faith. His influence is still being conveyed through his many students who are now professors in departments of religion and theological seminaries throughout this nation.

Richard Kroner is not an ordained minister. In Germany he was a lay member of the Prussian Union Church; in America he has been identified primarily with Lutheranism. At Union Theological Seminary, however, he was asked to officiate at the chapel services and to address the Union community at worship. The addresses published in this volume are a selection from those he delivered in James Chapel at Union Theological Seminary from 1943 to 1955.

These addresses contain the germ of Professor Kroner's theology, and they are written with a transparency and a lucidity which make them genuine religious expressions. They are primarily sermons dealing each with a portion of the Holy Scriptures. Their content is the spontaneous outpouring of a sensitive soul who has the capacity to penetrate into the depths of faith and to convey a sense of the mystery, majesty, and unfathomable sublimity of the Holy God. These addresses reflect the substance of a humble man's faith—a faith tested within the crucible of life's frustrations and defeats, a faith bearing the scars of the Crucified, a faith possessing the vision of a victorious resurrection.

I wish to thank my wife, Rosemary Edwards Skinner, for her limitless patience and her untiring efforts in polishing the style of these manuscripts originally prepared for oral presentation.

JOHN E. SKINNER

Divinity School of the Protestant
Episcopal Church in Philadelphia
September, 1963

Table of Contents

1

Holy Love

Beloved, let us love one another: for love is of God; and every one that loveth is born of God, and knoweth God. He that loveth not knoweth not God; for God is love . . . and he that dwelleth in love dwelleth in God, and God in him.

—I John 4:7, 8, 16

These words have a gentle sound; indeed they have almost too gentle a sound in our hate-torn world. How can we love God, if he is the Creator of this horrible world; and if he is love, how can he be the Creator of such a world? Are we not obliged to choose between that God who alone seems to be the real God, the Creator of this real world, and that God who is said to be love, and who therefore seems to be an unreal God, a God of our dreams only?

We would like to think that God is love; love makes us happy, while hate destroys us. But how can we sincerely trust the gentle message of our text when we see hate growing around the earth, and when greed and envy obviously prevail over charity and humility in the heart of man? In Nazi schools a primer is used which makes this statement: "The teaching of mercy and love of one's neighbor is foreign to the German race, and the Sermon on the Mount is, according to Nordic sentiments, an ethic for cowards and idiots." Is the teaching of mercy and love foreign to the German race alone or isn't it rather foreign to man in general, to man as he really is? Isn't the ethic of the Sermon on the Mount altogether unnatural and beyond the capacity of earthly beings?

A truth asserts itself in these skeptical arguments. Corresponding to our deepest feelings, a wide gulf separates real life and the love of God. If there is a God, he cannot be of this world; he cannot be pleased by the spec-

tacle of hate and war; he must be sought beyond the
horizon of this sinful world. His truth which transcends
the limit of our earthly experience separates him from
this world. If the nature of the Creator could be simply
learned from the nature of his creation, the boundary line
between Creator and creation would dwindle. World and
God could be identified, as pantheism teaches. But then
God would cease to be God. No longer being ultimate,
he would become an ambiguous demon who like man is
both good and bad. The world as we know it would itself become ultimate. But because the world is not ultimate we long for God; and because the truth we find in
this world is a changing truth, we cannot be satisfied
with it. Thus the contrast between the world and God
agrees with our deepest experience.

A state religion like that of the Nazis wishes to cancel
this contrast. It touches only the worldly side of our experience; yet unquestionably our experience needs integra-
tion and redemption through the holy love of the living
God. The Nazi creed hates the God of love. But we cannot hate God, because if we do, we admit that we love
the world as it is; that we do not long for a higher truth;
that we are satisfied with the state of hate and war, with
the cruelties of the tyrant and with the injustice of the
dictators. We must choose between this world and God.
But of course it is not true that we ourselves choose, because it is actually God who chooses us. If we know him,
we must love him, for he is love, and "he that loveth
not, knoweth not God."

But is not God the supreme judge over all our deeds,

and even over all our thoughts? Does he not know all our frailty and all our defects? Does he not condemn our heart because he knows it, and does he not know it even better than we ourselves? Is he therefore not to be feared more than to be loved? How can we love him who punishes us, before whom we must die of shame? How are we entitled to love him when he is so infinitely superior to us that we can never reach the light where he sits in majesty? "The Lord reigneth; let the people tremble" (Ps. 99:1). Is not trembling and fear the only adequate attitude of man toward God? And is this fear not related to hate? "Verily every man at his best state is altogether vanity" (Ps. 39:5). How can we, being the men we really are, dare to love the Almighty who has created and is creating all things? Does not love level him who loves and him who is loved? How can we dare to enter such an intimate and close alliance with him who alone is holy and perfect and therefore utterly remote from us? "Who shall ascend into the hill of the Lord? or who shall stand in his holy place?" (Ps. 24:3).

This prerogative is precisely the miraculous strength of the person who believes in Christ. This is the content of the Christian message, even though it seems incredible and embarrassing to the understanding that man in all his vanity and nullity should have access to the highest throne.

We can fear God—nay, we must fear him. But we can never hate him, for he is love. We may hate our neighbor, if he has insulted or injured us; we may hate the world, if we are persecuted or tortured by it; we may hate ourselves, if we feel the deficiency of our characters. But we can never hate God. We can forget who he is, we can fail to respond to the depths of his unfathomable mystery, but we can never hate him. It is true that we are not always aware of him; on the contrary, in the ordinary course of our daily lives even if we are called upon to serve him, we often estrange ourselves from him; we ignore his demand upon us. But even then we do not hate him. Should we ever fall so far away from him that we ceased to love him, then we would no longer know him at all. If we ever could hate him, then we would extol error and evil, and we would betray ourselves as loving lies and crimes the way the Nazis do. But then we would stop being children of God or even human beings.

We do not fathom the mystery of holy love; we should not even want to fathom it. It is the Unfathomable that we love when we love God; this mystery alone can redeem us from the sinful world. God would not be God if he were like visible things that surround us. If he were not mysterious and ineffable, he would not be the refuge from the hate that rages in the world. The contrast between world and God seems to be of the very essence of faith. A world that would not challenge our hearts, a world that could be fully and completely comprehended by scientific means, would be a world without God, without hate, and without love. As the contrast between good and evil is the precondition of good, thus the opposition between the sinful world and the holy God is the very precondition for the existence of God. We must accept this opposition if we long for God. Only a world that needs redemption can be redeemed by God. Only a world in which hate and enmity rage can evoke the love of God.

We love God because he is the mystery that frees us from the hate of the world. We love him because we hate ourselves, since it is our fault that the world is full of hate. But the love of God can perform the miracle of making us love even the hateful world and ourselves. When we love the world alone, we must hate God who is love: "If any man love the world, the love of the Father is not in him" (I John 2:15). We must therefore choose. We must love either the world or God; there is no other possibility. "Ye are of God, little children, and have overcome [the world]: because greater is he that is in you, than he that is in the world" (I John 4:4).

II

The Still, Small Voice

And the same day, when the even was come, he saith unto them, Let us pass over unto the other side. And when they had sent away the multitude, they took him even as he was in the ship. . . . And there arose a great storm of wind, and the waves beat into the ship, so that it was now full. And he was in the hinder part of the ship, asleep on a pillow: and they awake him, and say unto him, Master, carest thou not that we perish? And he arose, and rebuked the wind, and said unto the sea, Peace, be still. And the wind ceased, and there was a great calm. And he said unto them, Why are ye so fearful? how is it that ye have no faith? And they feared exceedingly, and said one to another, What manner of man is this, that even the wind and the sea obey him?

—Mark 4:35-41

Two different kinds of fear appear in this story. The disciples fear, first of all, the great storm of wind that threatens the ship and endangers their lives. "Master," they say, "carest thou not that we perish?" It is their natural life, their very existence about which they are anxious. "Why are ye so fearful?" Jesus answers. "How is it that ye have no faith?" Faith can overcome the anxiety a man may feel in the struggle for his existence when he is surrounded by dangerous powers that threaten to destroy his life. Faith generates courage, and courage is most important for the victory over hostile elements. Jesus evokes courage by the spiritual power of his personality, and courage overcomes the dangers of the hour.

Courage is a moral strength, but it also mobilizes the physical powers of man in his combat with natural elements. And thus indirectly it is even a physical energy. But before physical strength can be mustered, faith has to master the passion of fear. This passion is the echo of the storm of wind within the souls of the disciples; it is a tumult in their own breasts. Jesus masters and subdues this inner agony by his encouraging words. He is able to calm the sea because he is able to calm the souls. He can do it because his own soul is absolutely calm and absolutely serene in the face of both the raging of the outer wind and the fever of the inner passion. One incident in the story illustrates his complete moral and spiritual serenity. While the storm rages and the men are stricken with fear, Jesus is so indifferent to the danger that he sleeps quietly on a pillow in the stern of the ship until his disciples awake him.

The response to his appeal is not only the disappearance of the fear of the disciples, however, but also the rise of another fear. "And they feared exceedingly, and said one to another, What manner of man is this, that even the wind and the sea obey him?" Their physical anxiety had been smoothed away only to make room for a new and even greater passion. The Greek text does not use the same word for fear in both places. In the first passage the word "fearful" means cowardly or craven, but in the second passage the Greek says literally: "they feared a great fear." This great fear is not cowardice; it is fear of a different type. The word fear is used twice here in order to emphasize the intensity of that second fear which arose when the disciples saw that the words of Jesus spoken to the wind and the waves ("Peace, be still") were really obeyed by the elements of nature.

This second fear no longer concerns the physical danger that threatens the life of the sailors. Now they are frightened because their master, being a man like themselves, nevertheless seems to possess a superhuman power: "What manner of man is this that even the wind and the sea obey him?" This second fear is a kind of wonder provoked by the spiritual superiority and divine calm of Jesus. But the disciples do not recognize this fear for what it really is; they are stricken by terror because they cannot distinguish between divine power and magical or demonic power.

The question of Jesus, "Why are ye so fearful? How is it that ye have no faith?" seems to be related both to the cowardice caused by the physical danger and to the half-superstitious uneasiness aroused by his divinity. Jesus was saying: You should not fear the elements of nature, for the spirit is greater than nature, and you should not fear spiritual power, for you yourselves are of the spirit. The spirit is your own greatest strength. If you had the right faith, you would worship God in spirit and in truth, and thus you would overcome both your natural passions and your superstitious dread. You would know that God masters nature, outside man, precisely because he masters the passions inside man. You would understand that a devout heart can defeat and cast away all kinds of fear.

The situation of mankind today has some resemblance to the situation of the men in the ship on the Sea of Galilee. A storm has arisen as great as any that ever arose before in history; the waves beat into the ship of human civilization and endanger the existence of us all. And we ask, as the disciples did: "Master, carest thou not that we perish?" And we are reminded by the story not to be anxious but to trust in the help of that superior power who can say to the storm and to the sea: "Peace, be still." We should not expect a magical intervention that would smooth the earthquake by half-spiritual and half-physical means, arousing in us a superstitious and not a real and pure faith. Christ cannot soften the storm of history except by softening the passions of cowardice and terror in the life of man.

As in the ship on the Sea of Galilee, Christ was asleep

on a pillow when the storm broke out and raged, so it seems that God does not care about the storm of history caused by the elemental passions of man. We must awaken him by asking him for help. He is neither a natural nor a historical power; he is superior to both of them. Compared with the robust energy of material processes and with the equally vigorous energy of human passions he is amazingly weak. He is powerful and victorious only in the spiritual realm, because this is his realm and man must enter it to become aware of his infinite sovereignty. Here he is not only powerful, but almighty. From his throne he rules over nature and history. The Lord is not in the great and strong wind that rends the mountains, nor in the earthquake nor in the fire, but he speaks with a still, small voice. (See I Kings 19:11.) We must listen to that still, small voice in order to feel his overwhelming majesty.

III

Faith and Life's Conflicts

And it came to pass after these things, that God did tempt Abraham, and said unto him, Abraham: and he said, Behold, here I am. And he said, Take now thy son, thine only son Isaac, whom thou lovest, and get thee into the land of Moriah; and offer him there for a burnt offering upon one of the mountains which I will tell thee of.

—Genesis 22:1-2

The appalling story of Abraham's temptation and trial has been interpreted again and again, but it always remains bewildering and obscure. Although historical explanations of several kinds can be given, they do not touch upon the meaning of the story. Kierkegaard in one of his most profound books (*Fear and Trembling*) has made this meaning the subject of a psychological and theological analysis. It may be boldness to renew his attempt in a brief form, but the meaning of biblical stories is inexhaustible. Every new experience, every new epoch discloses new aspects.

Readers of the story will continue to be amazed and even upset by the way in which God tempts his good servant. Why does he demand this piteous sacrifice from Abraham? Why does he command the father to deprive himself of his most beloved son? This is an ordeal a thousand times more dreadful even than the fate of Job, who was deprived of his sons by the Holy God.

The gloomy tone of this trial is not obliterated by the final outcome, the repeal of God's demand and the blessing of Abraham; it cannot be dismissed any more than the somber character of Job's story can, by the final restoration of all his goods. As Kierkegaard enlarges upon the biblical report, Isaac might have lost forever his confidence in his father in consequence of the shock he had to suffer; he was well aware of the danger threatening him. In verse seven it is related that he asked his father: "Where is the lamb for a burnt offering?" And Abraham himself, although he willingly obeyed the stern command of the Lord, might have become so terrified that he never recovered from this sad experience.

Why does God apply this cruel and ferocious method in testing the strength of Abraham's faith? Why does he torture the heart of this just man to the utmost? Why does he tempt him in a way that might almost be called immoral, if we judged it by human concepts? Why does he jeopardize the high spiritual value of Abraham's fatherly love, although he intends to bless this love later on? Jesus prays, "Lead us not into temptation." But here we see before us the most gruesome, the most pitiless kind of temptation that can be imagined. We dream sometimes of ghastly situations similar to that in which Abraham is involved; we face the alternative to sacrifice either our good conscience or one of our nearest and dearest, and then we awake and thank God that it was only a dream and nothing else. But here it is God himself who forces a man to make his anxious decision by daylight and in full reality. How can we reconcile this almost diabolical temptation with the goodness and righteousness of the eternal God?

The story hints at a dark and tragic reality. Severe and unavoidable tensions between divergent values and duties thrust themselves into our lives. The love of the father toward his son and the love of man toward the Father of us all are contrasted in the trial of Abraham. The question is: if these two affections contradict one another, which is to be subordinated? One thinks of the saying of Jesus (Luke 14:26): "If any man come to me, and hate not his father, and mother, and wife, and children, and brethren, and sisters, yea, and his own life also, he cannot be my disciple." This is as hard a word as the dilemma allotted to Abraham by God. It seems as if both the story in Genesis and the saying of Jesus would pronounce the same fundamental truth: there is a hierarchy of values and duties, and there are collisions between lower and higher ones, and when such conflicts occur, man has to make his anxious and painful choice. Precisely in such situations are we tempted and tested!

Life abounds with conflicts and desperate decisions like the one in which Abraham is entangled. It is his almost incomprehensible moral and spiritual grandeur which causes him not to ponder or waver for a minute. With perfect calm he makes his choice. It does not appear that he even makes a choice at all. He simply obeys the divine challenge, as if no battle has taken place in his heart, as if it is a matter of course to slay his son with his own hand when God commands. The love of God ranks highest in the order of loyalties. In fact, this love ranks so high that it completely annuls any other affection, regardless how deeply rooted it may be or how far-reaching the consequences of its disavowal may be.

This truth which lies at the bottom of the story stirs our minds today with a particular force. The present world conflict rends our hearts and tempts our wills in a manifold way. Family love, patriotism, and devotion to God may and certainly do collide, hourly and daily. Different loyalties vie with each other. Not every man is as strong, as steadfast, and as serene as Abraham was. We waver, we tremble, we are confused and embarrassed. If a choice must be made between the love of my country and the love of my son, or between the love of my country and the love of God, or as in the case of Abraham himself, between the love of God and the love of my son, I may feel uncertain and torn asunder. We may pray, as Jesus did, "Lead us not into temptation," but the fact is that world and life lead us continuously into temptation and throw us into utter embarrassment. We live in a severe and rigid school which trains us for an unknown destination.

Not all sufferings should be interpreted as punishments. The path upward as such is steep and harsh. The inner conflicts we encounter, the temptations implied in the decisions we make, the trials we have to undergo as a result of these decisions, although we may choose the higher values—all these often bitter and dismal experiences seem to point to one and the same ultimate purpose: a radical and ever increasing purification of the heart. Such purification of the heart prepares us for the final judgment and the last journey leading to our eternal home. The ways of God are not our ways, and his thoughts are impenetrable to our minds. But we are blessed by the promise that he who endureth to the end shall be saved.

The story of Abraham's temptation and trial receives its consummation in the New Testament, which teaches that God gave his own son to suffer and to die that man may be redeemed. Sacrifice is thus interpreted as the precondition of salvation and of eternal blessing.

IV

The New Dimension of the Soul

What shall it profit a man, if he shall gain the whole world, and lose his own soul? Or what shall a man give in exchange for his soul?

—Mark 8:36-37

An Address Delivered May 1, 1945
On the Occasion of the
Forming of the United Nations

These words can be applied to the soul of a nation as well as to that of an individual. The events of our time have furnished us with ample proof that a nation can lose her soul. A great nation, admired and respected among the nations of the world because of the creativity and depth of her spirit, wanted to gain the whole world by force, even at the risk of sacrificing her good name and her very honesty. No more impressive lesson has ever been given in history than the tragic drama that unfolded as the result of this amazing undertaking.

Enormous powers came to the fore, so that we were reminded of Milton's picture of Satan and his host. Germany did not gain the world, but she did lose her soul. She lost her soul the very day the fraud of the Reichstag fire was committed. Although everyone in Germany knew about it, no one dared to speak. She lost her soul when the first concentration camps were established. Although everyone in Germany knew about them also, no one dared to speak. The concentration camps, where thousands of persons' bodies were tortured and scourged to death, transformed the whole of Germany into a spiritual concentration camp where every single incarcerated soul was tortured and coerced into agony and despair. What did it profit Germany that she gained victories so triumphantly before the outbreak of the war and in its early stages?

What was given her in exchange for her soul, except vainglory, idolatry, and a short-lived pomp?

Now, another drama is unfolding before our eyes, a drama in which the destiny of all mankind is at stake. Again the whole world is to be gained, not by the conquest of one individual nation, but rather by a peaceful collaboration of all nations. This new enterprise is motivated not by greed and avarice, but by political wisdom; not by the lust for power, but by the intention to surrender power for the benefit of the whole world. We are permitted to see a great moment in history—the fulfillment of the age-old hopes of mankind. The nations strive to gain the world, so that their souls may live. After one of the darkest nights that ever befell civilization, after one of the saddest relapses into the cruelty and barbarity of prehistoric times, we now witness the rise of an age in which the highest aspiration of all times is going to take shape: a world community to comprise all human beings living around the globe, and to insure an order of law and justice resembling that order hitherto accomplished only within the framework of sovereign individual states.

The lofty dream of impractical saints like Augustine and the daring design of secluded thinkers like Kant may assume historic reality. Whose heart should not exult at such a prospect! What a contrast between the Nazi rallies at Nuremberg, where the spirit of hate was displayed, and the San Francisco Conference, where the spirit of good will is at work! What a great difference between the horrors of the concentration camps and the humane endeavor to find a common ground upon which all the nations of the world can build a lasting peace! No one contrasting these events can doubt where the better chance lies of gaining the whole world without losing the soul.

The magnificent attempt to establish an all-embracing political organization, however, should not blind our eyes to the nature of this hopeful project. We should not forget that the organization sought is a political one, exposed to all the shortcomings and defects from which sinful men can never escape. It is not the city of God that will be built, even if the negotiations in San Francisco should be crowned with full success. It is at best a step made by rivalrous and ambitious nations. Each will and even must guard her own interests, privileges, achievements, ideals, and systems, so that the outcome can only be a compromise. As Mr. Stettinius has warned: "To build upon a millennial idealism, however fine in theory, would be to build upon quicksand . . ."

What is quicksand to the sober politician is the very content of faith and the hope of every Christian soul. The immense wall between the political realities and the spiritual imagination underlying our faith is insurmountable. Not the solemn expectation of the whole world, not the enthusiasm of every peace-loving soul should obscure this fact. Otherwise we would again risk the danger of gaining the whole world and losing the soul. Jesus certainly was not a politician, and never thought of a world community like that planned at the Conference. He thought of the city of God, not of the city of man. The best organized political institution in the world can never replace nor prepare that kingdom for which he lived and gave his life.

Almost all of the sayings of Jesus reveal a new dimension of inwardness. The soul, not as the psychologist understands the word, but as the quoted words in the Gospel intend, was first discovered by him. Although the Old Testament also knows the soul and the inwardness of each man, a new dimension of the soul and a new depth is disclosed in the message of Jesus. "Take heed that the light which is in thee be not darkness." "Fear not them which kill the body, but are not able to kill the soul: but rather fear him which is able to destroy both soul and body in hell." These are new accents betraying a new meaning of the word soul. The God of the Old Testament was first of all the God of the chosen people, and then the God of all nations, but only secondarily the God of the single individual soul. The Father to whom Jesus prays is related first of all to the soul of Jesus, then to the soul of every man, but only secondarily is the Father the Lord of the nations.

When we look at the political scene as the place in which God primarily acts, we are falling back from the faith of the gospel to that of the old covenant. To be sure, the spirit of Christ should inspire us in all our doing, and certainly all our political energies should be imbued with the ultimate hopes which spring from our faith. But we should also be aware that there is this insurmountable wall between world and soul, between political history and spiritual imagination, and that we are always risking our souls when we try to gain the world. This happens even when prudent and diplomatic realism, clearly contrasted against naked and brutal force, is the conqueror; it also occurs when the wisdom and good will of all nations seeks for a peaceful world organization in contradistinction to the arrogance and selfishness of one nation.

When viewed from the political point of view, Jesus certainly was a millennial idealist who built upon quicksand. But seen from the spiritual point of view, he built his kingdom on the only indestructible rock and irretrievable ground: the ground of the human soul. For what shall a man give in exchange for his soul?

V

Holy Vengeance

Dearly beloved, avenge not yourselves, but rather give place unto wrath: for it is written, Vengeance is mine; I will repay, saith the Lord.

—Romans 12:19

In these days when the unspeakable crimes perpetrated by cruel tyrants are shocking the world, the problem of just retribution may be considered anew. The enormous misdeeds necessarily call forth the demand of retaliation. Especially those who have suffered personally from the hands of the bloody dictators cry out loudly for vengeance. This is natural, but the Lord warns us: "Vengeance is mine; I will repay," and the apostle comments: "Avenge not yourselves, but rather give place unto wrath."

Why are we forbidden to avenge ourselves, even when undeniable facts accuse and condemn the offender? Why are we not permitted to repay evil we have received unjustly? Can anything else make restitution for the violated law? And who can be better entitled to mete out just retribution than the one who knows best what effect the outrage of the lawbreaker has had, and consequently what should be the adequate measure of reprisal?

A simple consideration at once corrects this suggestion, natural though it is. Vengeance is evidently a dangerous incentive to retributive justice. Precisely because the victim of aggression and cruelty has suffered, he cannot be an impartial judge. Vengeance mostly is blind; in any case it is the outburst of excitement. No matter how justified the excitement may be, it is the explosion of a tormented soul. Just retribution should be the result of quiet investigation and balanced discernment. Vengeance is an act of passion, but a just verdict is an act of self-control-

31

ling reason. Vengeance therefore can by no means cure the evil which provoked it; it cannot re-establish the destroyed equilibrium of the moral order; it cannot recover the peace violated by the perpetrator.

Moreover, reprisals, which are exercised not by law but by passion, cannot end the tension between the persons or groups involved. Because the avenger acts in his own name, he does not act in the name of justice. Greek tragedy teaches us that a never-ending chain of charges and countercharges, of plots and counterplots, is the necessary outcome of retaliatory retribution which is motivated and enacted by the spirit of revenge. Vengeance, therefore, always produces new acts of vengeance.

Does the apostle think of orderly jurisdiction when he advises the Roman Christians not to avenge themselves? In the chapter that follows this advice he exalts the authority of governments and insists that it is ordained by God. He calls the magistrate a servant of God, and explicitly adds: "He is a revenger to execute wrath upon him that doeth evil," or in the translation of Professor Moffatt, "he is God's servant for the infliction of divine vengeance upon evildoers." Certainly, retribution carried out by a court of justice is more in accordance with the commandment of God than that done in passion.

Does this interpretation of the word "I will repay, saith the Lord" cover its deepest meaning? The criminal should be sentenced, but can a human sentence fully satisfy the demand of retribution? The wrath of God is a combination of passion and reason. It is passion, but being divine it is also in agreement with reason; it is reason, but being divine it is not cold legality, that is, a sober application of juridical terms; it is not the jurisdiction of the jurists. It is a passionate jurisdiction coming out of a warm heart. The wrath of God is distinguished from human passion by absolute impartiality. It is also distinguished from human reason by the partiality of a loving father who punishes his child. This combination brings about the divine perfection of justice.

If we seriously consider the question of which kind of punishment would be the adequate one in the case of culprits like Mussolini and Hitler whose crimes are crying to heaven, postulating the wrath of God we must answer that any penalty decreed by man would be utterly inadequate. Deeds so monstrous and so prodigious as those, which injured the freedom and happiness, the health and hopes of millions of innocent people, seem immeasurable. No measure taken by human courts, however hard and harsh, can correspond to the scientific brutality of the concentration camps. When the Italian partisans hanged the dead body of Mussolini in a public street, his head downwards, we felt this to be an incommensurate and helpless expression of the profoundly true insight that the execution alone did not satisfy the demand of just retribution.

What other penalty would satisfy this demand? If we carefully consider the question, we come to the following result: Only if it were possible to open the eyes and the hearts of men like Mussolini and Hitler and their henchmen to the gross reality of their guilt; if they could be made to experience the bottomless, heartbreaking misery they have inflicted, and if at the same time they could be made to comprehend fully the scope of their own responsibility so that the burden of their crimes fell back upon their own souls—only then would justice be restored and right retribution exacted. But, of course, this penalty would demand that they forswear all the arrogance and false conceit in which they have indulged; it would imply indeed that a new and truly human heart had been put in the empty shell of their breasts. This is the mystery of the holy vengeance and wrath of God: it entails an inner transformation of the soul. Only if the guilty man can fully measure the scope of his transgression does a hell of grief flame up in his heart. Just retribution is remorse; remorse itself is hell.

God and God alone can punish adequately, simply because he alone can transform the soul. God alone, with whom nothing is impossible, can achieve this wonder. He alone has the power to remove pride and to replace it by repentance. Without repentance the heart of the transgressor does not suffer remorse, and he does not live in that hell which corresponds to the reality of his transgression. Dante's picture of hell is deficient because he did not sufficiently understand this truth; the punishments, therefore, depicted by him do not appear quite adequate—they are not altogether worthy of the spirit of divine justice. God does not punish without purifying the heart; this very purification creates hell in the soul of the man who realizes what he has done. Just retribution brought about by the wrath of God brings the sinner back to God. God heals in punishing! "O the depth of the riches both of the wisdom and knowledge of God!"

The fire of hell consumes the dregs of the crimes. Hell, in the last analysis, is purgatory. Divine justice culminates in divine mercy. God the Avenger finally becomes God the Redeemer. This is the reason why God and God alone can restore the order broken by sin; why he alone can decree and promote that state of perfect peace which is the holy charter of the kingdom of heaven.

VI

Joy in Heaven

Then drew near unto him all the publicans and sinners for to hear him. And the Pharisees and scribes murmured, saying, This man receiveth sinners, and eateth with them. And he spake this parable unto them, saying, What man of you, having an hundred sheep, if he lose one of them, doth not leave the ninety and nine in the wilderness, and go after that which is lost, until he find it? And when he hath found it, he layeth it on his shoulders, rejoicing. And when he cometh home, he calleth together his friends and neighbors, saying unto them, Rejoice with me; for I have found my sheep which was lost. I say unto you, that likewise joy shall be in heaven over one sinner that repenteth, more than over ninety and nine just persons, which need no repentance.

—Luke 15.1-7

These words are by no means so self-evident as they may sound. To be sure, the contrast between the sinner and the Pharisee, the man who repents and the man who is too conceited and too self-righteous to feel the need of repentance, is familiar enough to us, and we may be prompted to substitute it for the contrast between the sinner who repents and the person who needs no repentance. This substitution, however, does not hit the mark either in the case of the parable or of the words which expound it. Jesus does not compare sinner and Pharisee; he contrasts those who need repentance and those who do not need it; he compares in other words the sinner and the truly just and righteous man who does not fail.

Why does Jesus prefer him who transgresses the commandments (even though he afterwards confesses his transgressions) to him who does not trangress at all and therefore does not need confession? Would not common sense rank higher the good-natured man who resists temptations rather than the man who falls into evil, though he later may feel remorse and be willing to repent? Does not Jesus himself teach us to pray: "Lead us not into temptation"? Is it not the goal of all moral striving and even of all politically sound planning to create a world in which depravity and wickedness of all kinds are completely eliminated so that no man need repent any more? Would not a world entirely void of all corruption, as we imagine the heavenly habitation of God and his angels to be, correspond better with our moral ideals than this world of ours in which sin persists and sinners need to repent? And yet, Jesus says there shall be greater joy in heaven over one sinner that repents than over ninety-nine righteous persons.

This observation is paradoxical indeed; it challenges moral reason; it may even upset moral judgments. We may argue that the exaltation of repentance endangers moral fortitude. People may deliberately sin if they are allowed to hope that their confession will please God more than all their steadfastness and continued continence can possibly do. We may conclude, therefore, that Jesus exaggerated the value of repentance and contrition to the degree of reversing the simple truth that not to sin is better than to sin and then to confess. His doctrine would indeed do more to provoke transgressions than to heal man and to help him avoid them.

We must look closer, however, at our text. Jesus does not say that the sinner is the better man if he repents. What he really says is that the joy over the repenting sinner exceeds the joy over ninety-nine just persons. This statement summarizes the parable of the good shepherd who loses one of his hundred sheep and leaves the ninety-nine in the open field and goes after the lost one until he finds it; then he rejoices when he has found the sheep that was lost. The parable more than the explanation which follows it illuminates the true meaning of the paradoxical observation. Jesus does not in any way intend to judge the repenting sinner by comparing him with the man of blameless conduct. Rather he rejoices that his own office and mission is that of the shepherd of mankind who "is come to save that which was lost." He has not come to call the righteous but to rescue the victims of Satan from the archenemy of mankind and of God. He rejoices at this victory over the power of evil and he feels that God also rejoices every time a soul is saved and Satan is defeated. Here Jesus does not intend to advise men how to behave; here he does not even admonish the sinner to repent, as he often does. Nor does he wish to comfort the man who is tormented by a bad conscience, by telling him that he pleases God.

Rather, Jesus is informing the disciples about the meaning of his work, and he incites them to perform the same mission by not condemning sinners but guiding them so that they may find their way back to the peace of their souls. The parable and its interpretation is accordingly a piece of instruction given to those who are supposed to take over the work Jesus has begun.

It should not be denied, however, that there are far-reaching consequences and deeper issues involved in this teaching. The joy felt in heaven over the penitent sinner is not without relation to the total mission of Jesus, and to the whole view of God and man as depicted in the Bible. Although Jesus does not intend to exalt the repenting sinner over the just man unduly, still he may point to the fact that man can never be completely just, and therefore he who would strive after faultlessness and blameless-ness is likely to become the victim of Satan as does the Pharisee who indulges in self-righteousness and in a com-placency which is an even worse frailty. His parable and his exposition thus may indirectly indicate that God loves more than the conceited Pharisee the sinner who is prepared to confess.

Finally, the deepest mystery at which the parable of the lost sheep seems to hint concerns the economy of God's salvation in its widest scope, beginning with the fall of Adam and ending in the redemption wrought by Jesus, the second Adam, who "is come to save that which was lost," and who is thereby the Christ. Jesus intimates in the imaginative form typical of his most momentous expressions that the fall is not only a culpable and therefore a regrettable and destructive misuse of man's free will, but also an event preordained by the supreme wisdom of the Creator. He seems to inform the disciples that sin is a mystery in that man cannot attain to the full stature and perfection of his character without transgression and the ensuing conversion.

The joy in heaven over repentance of one sinner is exuberant because this implies that at least one man approaches the ultimate goal of all men. Man has to turn away from God and he has to return to God. Only by this double movement can his soul be so purified and fortified as to be acceptable to the grace of God. Jesus participates in this supreme wisdom; he alone understands the secret plan of God. It is this impression which persuaded the disciples to recognize him as the Son of God, and which still today persuades the sensitive reader of the sayings of Jesus to recognize him as the divine wisdom incarnate—the Word of God made flesh.

VII

The Foolishness of God

For it is written, I will destroy the wisdom of the wise, and will bring to nothing the understanding of the prudent. Where is the wise? where is the scribe? where is the disputer of this world? hath not God made foolish the wisdom of this world? For after that in the wisdom of God the world by wisdom knew not God, it pleased God by the foolishness of preaching to save them that believe. For the Jews require a sign, and the Greeks seek after wisdom: but we preach Christ crucified, unto the Jews a stumblingblock, and unto the Greeks foolishness; but unto them which are called, both Jews and Greeks, Christ the power of God, and the wisdom of God. Because the foolishness of God is wiser than men; and the weakness of God is stronger than men.

—I Cor. 1:19-25

These familiar words may be among the most daring utterances of faith ever stated by any man. What audacity to speak of the foolishness of him in whom all wisdom is personified, to speak of the weakness of him who is invested with absolute power! These words appear all the more bold if we realize that Paul is not merely using a rhetorical phrase, but that he is in dead earnest. He does not merely mean that God is foolish in the eyes of the fool; no, God is foolishness when measured by the standards of human prudence and even of human wisdom. God is weak not only if weighed by false means of appraisal, but also if evaluated in a very real sense.

He who sets the rules for the movement of the stars, he who commands the storms and controls the oceans and the streams, he whose majesty and sovereignty is unrestricted and unrestrained could not prevent his own beloved son from being despised and repudiated, tormented, and ultimately put to death. He did not choose kings or statesmen or any other authorities to enact his purpose, but he selected a man who was given over to an utterly unjust and cruel tribunal. He whose judgment never errs, and whose insight never fails, trusted the most simple people in order to reveal to them his most profound truths. He did not choose scientists, philosophers or even theologians as teachers of mankind in matters most sublime and most hidden; he chose poor unlearned fishermen as his disciples.

From the point of view of human understanding God is weak and foolish. History and common experience seem to corroborate what Paul says. The atheists, the naturalists, the pragmatists would not be able to sprout so abundantly and flourish in our world, if God were strong enough to suppress his enemies. But he is so far removed from suppressing them that he seems rather to encourage them in giving excessive illustrations to prove his nonexistence. It is easier to explain or expound the morally repulsive facts and features of life if we assume that no moral being rules, than it is if we assume that a moral ruler exists.

What the atheists do not see, however, is the possibility that our human standards may be wrong; that the weakness of God may be stronger than men, and that the foolishness of God may be wiser than men. What they do not see is the hidden power of a childlike love and the hidden wisdom of a childlike imagination. God's wisdom is foolish if we expect it to be in agreement with our scientific, our rational, our logical ideals and methods; it is foolish if we compare his deeds and procedures with our diplomatic and political habits and maxims, if we suppose that he has human understanding and human thoughts. And God's power is slight, indeed, if we measure it in terms of physical or technical, military or economic resources. What is weaker than a childlike love in the struggle of nations, in the combat of soldiers, in the conversations of ambassadors or delegates of states; what is more inadequate in ascertaining truth or in finding out the most prudent way of acting than a childlike imagination! And yet, the wisdom of God and the power of God resemble more closely that imagination and that love than they do the most refined and exact means of scientific observation and the best equipped army or police force. Scientists may receive an answer from the moon and other celestial bodies, but they will never manage to contact celestial souls. And even the atom bomb will always be weaker than the word of God and the love of Christ.

We must become like little children, then, in order to understand the power and wisdom of God and in order to follow Christ. We must surrender our wisdom, and we must relinquish our ideas of government, of influence, of ambition, and of aspiration. We ourselves must become foolish in the eyes of the world so that our eyes may see what the merely intelligent and prudent can never see. And we ourselves must become weak in the eyes of the world, so that our hearts may feel what the powerful and the mighty and those in authority rarely feel.

Such a surrender of our intellectual pride and of our practical interests contradicts our natural tendencies and even our moral self-assertion and self-assurance. It shakes the foundations of our normal life, as we live in the midst of the struggles and the tumult of the world. It is hard to combine both the prudence necessary in the affairs of our daily life and the simplicity demanded by God; to reconcile the humility of Christ with the toughness of resolve demanded by our purposes and even by the moral duties arising out of our place in the world. It is hard, in other words, to reconcile our human wisdom to the foolishness of God and our human capacity to the weakness of God.

Two kinds of temptation promise to release us from this inner tension. We can emphasize in our inward coucil the importance of our human morality and guard ourselves against the foolishness of a simple soul and the weakness of a meek will. We can give priority to the pressing interests and obligations of the hour and push the wisdom and the glory of God backward to the farthest edge of our practical life. Then we may at the end stiffen in our moral attitude to the point where we are endangered by self-righteousness and either stoic or pharisaic self-sufficiency. Or we can yield to the contrary temptation. We can labor to live as monks, though the world is not relinquished in a monastery. We can try to forget the battles of the day, we can shut our eyes to the arena of strife and dream of perfectionism and of sanctity. We may at the end really lose contact not only with the world, but also with ourselves, and submit to the human foolishness of self-deceit and to the human weakness of sentimentalism.

We must avoid both temptations. We can never become as powerful and as wise as we would like to become, humanly speaking; we can never become as foolish and weak as God and Christ. We must restrict our natural tendencies, although we are not allowed to suppress them completely. We must maintain our human strength and prudence, yet we must not allow them to fill our whole souls and to destroy our spiritual imagination and our childlike hope, love, and faith. We cannot accomplish this difficult and arduous task without the guidance and support of God.

VIII

The Day of the Lord

And Jesus went out, and departed from the temple: and his disciples came to him for to shew him the buildings of the temple. And Jesus said unto them, See ye not all these things? verily I say unto you, There shall not be left here one stone upon another, that shall not be thrown down. And as he sat upon the mount of Olives, the disciples came unto him privately, saying, Tell us, when shall these things be? and what shall be the sign of thy coming, and of the end of the world? And Jesus answered and said unto them, Take heed that no man deceive you. For many shall come in my name, saying, I am Christ; and shall deceive many. And ye shall hear of wars and rumours of wars: see that ye be not troubled: for all these things must come to pass, but the end is not yet. For nation shall rise against nation, and kingdom against kingdom: and there shall be famines, and pestilences, and earthquakes, in divers places. All these are the beginning of sorrows. Then shall they deliver you up to be afflicted, and shall kill you: and ye shall be hated of all nations for my name's sake. And then shall many be offended, and shall betray one another, and shall hate one another. And many false prophets shall rise, and shall deceive many. And because iniquity shall abound, the love of many shall wax cold. But he that shall endure unto the end, the same shall be saved.

—Matt. 24:1-13

If Jesus had spoken these prophetic statements to recent followers, his words could not have been more timely. They seem to refer directly to events that we have seen with our own eyes, to circumstances still prevailing in the world. It is as if Jesus had sat in the center of Berlin before the war, surrounded by many Christian churches and other monumental buildings, and had said to the German pastors: "See ye not all these things? Verily I say unto you, there shall not be left here one stone upon another, that shall not be thrown down." And now again we hear rumors of war and we witness famines of an extent and a gravity hardly ever experienced before. We wonder if the end of the world is coming. Eschatological feelings are no longer a rarity confined to a small group of ecstatic believers; they have become our daily mood. We are, in fact, expecting something akin to the end of the world, of our world, of the world in which history has taken place for thirty centuries.

The idea of such an end is no longer fantastic. It has entered the stage of sober discussions; it has impregnated the consciousness even of the most realistic and uninspired people. Prophecy has turned into politics, and ecstasy has been transformed into tough deliberations about the most pressing problems of the future. The issue is no longer which nation may outgrow the others; the issue is: Will mankind outgrow another war, or has the end come?

Disciples of Christ, therefore, are in severe trouble. We

have seen them persecuted in many lands, and the words
of Jesus have been literally fulfilled: "Then shall they
deliver you up to be afflicted, and shall kill you: and ye
shall be hated . . . for my name's sake." In the heart of
Christendom there is an appalling decrease of real Christians. In many of them love has grown cold and they
hate one another. But Jesus says to his disciples: Be not
alarmed, all this has to come before you will see me
again. Why must affliction and revolt, disloyalty and
devastation, hate and persecution, take place before the
end actually comes? Why are the disciples to be in deadly
anguish and hopelessness and troubles of all kinds before they are permitted to see Christ again? Why must a
general uproar, a formidable doom, a state of universal
distrust, and an alarming threat precede the final advent
of the kingdom of God? Is this prophecy entirely arbi-
trary? Is it mystical in the sense that it cannot be comprehended by any means? Is it a fact simply to be ac-
cepted because it is ordained by the highest and holiest
authority? Or are we permitted to lift the veil of this
mystery, at least to a certain degree?

Since we are eyewitnesses of this tremendous process,
we can at least ponder on the circumstances which have
brought about the enormous crisis of our civilization. We
know something about its inner history, about our own
feelings and standards before it broke out, and about the
reaction of our souls after it erupted. We know that a
period of apparent security, increase of wealth, and belief
in the potentiality of technical and industrial production
precipitated the present disaster. We know that the eight-

eenth and nineteenth centuries surpassed all the other periods of Western civilization in the immensity of their human achievements in the realm of science as well as in developing scientific devices useful for the needs and wants of men. We know that this unique progress made man believe he was on the way to absolute perfection; no longer did he have to fear the adversity of subhuman elements, for the mind of man could investigate them all, discovering their secrets and eventually subduing them to the will of man. We know that the success of these investigations blinded and intoxicated even the critically and skeptically minded, and that few could completely resist this alluring view of *human* hope. The day of the Lord no longer seemed remote, but it was not the day of the Lord longed for by Christian believers; it was rather the day of the scientist that outshone all other hopes. The kingdom of God seemed to have drawn near, but it was not the kingdom of Christ so long awaited; rather it was the kingdom of the engineer, which was to have the same salutary effect and to cure all human evils.

But now we are driven out from all these vainglorious dreams. A paradise of illusions has been lost. It was a fool's paradise. Man had been deceived by his own accomplishments, by his own triumphs. The real, the immortal, the divine truth has expressed itself once more. It is precisely this disappointment with our own resources, our own successes, our own intellectual victories which has opened our eyes to the resources of the eternal victor. We have learned or are going to learn that we must ultimately surrender all our arrogance and all our pretension to the power of him who is without arrogance and pretension because he is the real Lord of our life. From all the disasters, miseries, crimes, and sorrows of our days, we have learned or are going to learn that our own efforts and works, our own power and ingenuity is fruitless. And worse, it is even dangerous; it will destroy us in the end, if the spirit of the Lord, the spirit of grace and love, does not help us to overcome the otherwise invincible and indomitable enemies of mankind: envy and greed, lust of power, self-indulgence, and self-righteousness.

We know from within ourselves that there is a close connection between the tribulations and sufferings prophesied by Jesus and the advent promised by him. We know from within ourselves that we have to be castigated in order to turn our hearts and souls to God; that we have to despair of our own strength in order to rely upon the strength of him who alone can kindle the flame of divine love in our hearts. The collapse of Western civilization has to precede the rise of the kingdom of God. The end of the world is an ambiguous expression; it means the end of the reign of man and the coming of the day of the Lord. It means the decline of man's autonomous and self-sufficient world and the dawn of the Eternal Glory. "Of old hast thou laid the foundation of the earth: and the heavens are the work of thy hands. They shall perish, but thou shalt endure: yea, all of them shall wax old like a garment. . . . But thou art the same, and thy years shall have no end" (Ps. 102:25–27).

IX

Holy Intolerance

Whosoever therefore shall confess me before men, him will I confess also before my Father which is in heaven. But whosoever shall deny me before men, him will I also deny before my Father which is in heaven. Think not that I am come to send peace on earth: I came not to send peace, but a sword. For I am come to set a man at variance against his father, and the daughter against her mother, and the daughter in law against her mother in law. And a man's foes shall be they of his own household. He that loveth father or mother more than me is not worthy of me: and he that loveth son or daughter more than me is not worthy of me. And he that taketh not his cross, and followeth after me, is not worthy of me. He that findeth his life shall lose it: and he that loseth his life for my sake shall find it. He that receiveth you receiveth me, and he that receiveth me receiveth him that sent me.

—Matt. 10:32-40

Words so often read and heard as these tend gradually to lose the appalling and alarming severity, the threatening and awful tone, originally connected with them. Habit assuages their harshness. But the moment that we take them seriously, we discover how utterly incapable we are of living in accordance with their stern command. Not many of us are prepared to testify sincerely that we would sacrifice everything to the service of God, or that we would desire a life only in and for Christ. Not many of us would be able to surrender every bond without compromise, even that which is most dear, most sweet, most intimate, should it preclude that perfect submission to the demand of Jesus. Most of us, I suppose, would feel obliged to confess that we do not know whether we should be strong enough in the hour of trial to respond to the challenge which the words imply.

It is probably easier to die for a cause than it is to live without finding one's life, to live and yet abandon everything that we esteem and love should the hour require it for the sake of Christ. It is certainly easier to keep peace with those we encounter, even if they are not truly devoted to the cause of Christ, than to draw the sword and to war against them. But Jesus says: "I came not to send peace, but a sword." He permits no compromise whatsoever. He does not allow friendship between one who confesses him and one who denies him, not even within the same family. Most of us are appeasers of some kind, in some field, to some degree. Most of us feel the security of peace so strongly that we should not be able to risk that absolute and perfect devotion [to Christ] which might lead to a breach in a valuable relationship, and end in bitter conflict.

At times we even hear the gospel expounded in terms of compromise for the sake of peace. Christian love and tolerance seem to be so intrinsically connected that they are often confused. Religious tolerance is one of the tenets sacred to democracy. But we should not forget, and should not veil the fact, that it is not at all sacred to those who follow Christ. These words of Jesus do not imply religious tolerance. They express, on the contrary, his strict and stubborn command to reject even the most lofty human emotions and loyalties, when his cause is at stake. That cause, as a source of antagonism, might well shatter all our relations and obligations, all our affections and considerations. The whole compass of human feelings and interests must be denied, when Christ summons us. "He that findeth his life shall lose it." In those words, Christ admits no exception, no possibility of compromise. He does not tolerate tolerance.

Is not this kind of intolerance dangerous? Is it not amenable to an interpretation which might provoke the most sinister consequences? It is formidable to think that Christ came not to bring peace, but a sword, that he came not to reconcile, but to divide, that he came to set man against man, especially within the relationships of a home. If that is the consequence of his words—and it seems difficult to evade such a conclusion—the door to all kinds of fanaticism and persecution is obviously opened. The horrors of religious hatred, despotism, inquisition, and cruelty seem to be foreshadowed and sanctified by the intolerance recommended, even demanded, by these words. History shows that they really served, or at least did not prevent, all the outrages both of the Roman Catholic and of the Protestant churches, committed in the name of, and for the sake of, Christ. It is evident, however, that these consequences are a mere mockery of the purpose of Christ and of the message of the kingdom of heaven. For the kind of intolerance that Jesus demands is not to be confused with human disputes and dissensions, dogmatic or otherwise.

The fanaticism of modern dictatorships, moreover, warns us not to misinterpret Christ's holy intolerance. Leaders like Hitler and Mussolini exacted from their followers an obedience and devotion that were as absolute and boundless as the religious obedience and devotion demanded by Jesus. He who has dwelt under a totalitarian regime is familiar with the hideous and detestable symptoms of a pseudoreligious zealotism. He knows what an agony life is when families are divided against themselves; when a father can no longer trust his son; when a husband cannot trust his wife, and a brother cannot trust his brother, because the sword of the dictator has destroyed their peace; when all bonds of friendship are dissolved, because the chains imposed by the leader permit no private affections; when all human relationships are exclusively controlled by the excessive, all-embracing authority of a self-styled savior of a nation. It is then, in truth, that a man's enemies are of his own household.

Countries misguided and finally demolished by gangsters, however, can as little illustrate or disparage the idea of an absolute religious devotion as can the heinous atrocities of a despotic church. We cannot compare the poisoned weapons of the fascists or the insidious tribunals of the Inquisition with the sword of Jesus, which is as gentle as it is exacting. We cannot and should not compare the cause of ruthless and arrogant fanatics with the cause for which our Lord lived and died. For there is one cause and one cause only which can command absolute surrender and perfect obedience, and which can justify all the consequences of an inflexible and uncompromising loyalty. That cause is the cause of God himself, and the one which Jesus Christ represented. The stiff and inexorable language he uses in his alarming address mirrors the ultimacy and majesty of the highest judge, the Creator and Lord of all life. "He that receiveth me receiveth him that sent me." Nothing deserves to be acknowledged, and indeed nothing can be tolerated, which opposes that supreme cause. Only those human relationships which are compatible with that cause have genuine value. No excess or fanaticism is possible when it is at stake. For human relations reach their fulfillment, truth, and perfection only when the law of God lives within the human heart, and only when all his children know him. Then all intolerance is replaced by love, and this is the only way to put an end to intolerance.

But the time of the new government has not yet come. Our future will certainly abound in struggles which may require an attitude of harsh sternness like that of our Lord's frightening words. Although our last centuries have been great so far as human civilization is concerned, they have also been periods of religious indifference and appeasement. The Christian nations seemed to have achieved a reconciliation, at least a certain equilibrium, between their secular life and God's holy commandments. But no longer does that reconciliation seem valid. We have entered a period of history in which religious tolerance is in danger of becoming a betrayal of Christ. We must consider anew the gravity of the words of Jesus, for a new paganism has arisen and is still arising. It is flooding the countries where Christian civilization has flourished for centuries. A savage and cynical denial of the very ideal for which Jesus suffered, and to which his disciples were summoned, is sweeping the world. The hearts of men are shattered by the very split to which Jesus points in his harsh words. We approach a time in which it may be very difficult to maintain the fine and delicate line between a comfortable but inexcusable indifference and appeasement, and a firm but formidable fanaticism. And yet, this delicate line must be found and maintained, for upon it alone can the peace of God eventually replace the sword of Christ. It is in such a time as ours that the ultimate test of Christian loyalty can again assume the value it possessed during the earliest centuries of the Christian faith.

X

The Generosity of God

*Therefore is the kingdom of heaven likened unto a
certain king, which would take account of his servants.
And when he had begun to reckon, one was brought
unto him, which owed him ten thousand talents. But
forasmuch as he had not to pay, his lord commanded
him to be sold, and his wife, and children, and all that
he had, and payment to be made. The servant therefore
fell down, and worshipped him, saying, Lord, have
patience with me, and I will pay thee all. Then the
Lord of that servant was moved with compassion, and
loosed him, and forgave him the debt. But the same
servant went out, and found one of his fellowservants,
which owed him an hundred pence: and he laid hands
on him, and took him by the throat, saying, Pay me that
thou owest. And his fellowservant fell down at his feet,
and besought him, saying, Have patience with me, and
I will pay thee all. And he would not: but went and
cast him into prison, till he should pay the debt. So
when his fellowservants saw what was done, they were
very sorry, and came and told unto their lord all that
was done. Then his lord, after that he had called him,
said unto him, O thou wicked servant, I forgave thee
all that debt, because thou desiredst me: Shouldest not
thou also have had compassion on thy fellowservant,
even as I had pity on thee? And his lord was wroth,
and delivered him to the tormentors, till he should pay
all that was due unto him. So likewise shall my heavenly
Father do also unto you, if ye from your hearts forgive
not every one his brother their trespasses.*

—Matt. 18:23-35

Some puzzling features assert themselves in this parable. It could be argued that Jesus, in making divine forgiveness depend upon man's first forgiving his fellow man, depicts God's grace as given not freely but on the condition of human merit, thus restricting the sovereignty and freedom of God's redemptive act. Such dogmatic reasoning forgets that although God forgives the sinner without taking human merit into account, he nevertheless does not forgive without condition. One indispensable condition must be fulfilled: the sinner must respond to God's offer by an attitude of his heart which demonstrates that he is willing to accept the gift of God's grace. This attitude would necessarily lead him to forgiveness of his fellow men as described in the parable. A person is a believer and a follower of Christ only if he is prepared to practice clemency in all his relations to other persons. Jesus teaches us, therefore, to pray: "Forgive us our debts, as we forgive our debtors." In these words, our forgiveness is not the condition but the presupposition of our prayers for God's forgiveness.

Many other questions which are not so easily answered may be raised by the simile of the sinner as debtor of God. In what sense and to what degree can God's act of redemptive love be compared to the renunciation of legal claims? Or, if we drop the juridical symbol of the parable, in what way is God's remission of sins to be understood in comparison to an act of human compassion and leniency? What is the limit of this compassion? It is obvious from the outset that some line should be drawn between the divine and the human kind of forgiveness, between the remission of sins by the Savior and the remission of debts by a human creditor, even if we do not interpret the word "debts" in a legal sense. God's claims on man are infinitely higher than any individual's claims on his fellow man; as a result, God's forgiveness should be understood as infinitely more powerful.

In order to find the difference between the two kinds of forgiveness, we should proceed by comparing the nature of the different claims made by God and by man. Man is indebted to God in that he owes God obedience, reverence, and love, and because as a sinner he has not paid what he should pay. He is disobedient, irreverent, and in revolt against the will and the commandments of the Creator and Lord. Similarly the debtor is indebted to his human creditor, because he has not done what he should have done. This tremendous difference, however, can be discerned between the divine and the human claimant: God's property, if we may use this expression, is not involved when he claims the right attitude of the sinner toward nim. His wealth, his power, his resources are not diminished by the unpaid debts of man, for God and man are never on the same level. God cannot be deprived of his inalienable rights; he cannot be offended; he cannot be injured. Rather it is man who deprives himself of the highest right given to him when he destroys the covenant between the Creator and himself by his sin. It is man who offends himself and injures himself by revolting against his Lord. What God claims is for the benefit and welfare not of himself, but of man. Not God, but sinful man, profits from paying his debts to the greatest benefactor and protector of our welfare.

Consequently, the meaning of forgiveness must vary. When a creditor cancels the debts of his debtor, or when a judge shows mercy to a transgressor, or when someone pardons his offender, the act of forgiveness betrays a certain generosity, insofar as the creditor waives his claims, the judge waives his juridical power, and the offended person waives vengeance and satisfaction. Such generosity does not obliterate the fault or guilt of the culprit. It does grant him a certain favor, but this favor does not reach the guilty conscience; it cannot restore the inner integrity of the transgressor although it may restore his place in society or his honor, or even comfort his heart and add something to his happiness. The generosity of man is not the generosity of God, and the effect of human forgiveness does not equal that of God's forgiving grace in the remission of sins.

God does not renounce his claims when he pardons the sinner, and yet his generosity is incomparably greater. The sinner has forfeited all his rights. He has destroyed the bond with him to whom man owes all. The favor he is granted is no less than the restitution of his very humanity, the noblest and most precious gift a person can receive. While human clemency restores mere outer goods, God's grace enters into the innermost citadel of the person—his conscience. Only the unique act of God can perform this mystery. He alone can permeate the human soul, because he has created that soul, and he alone knows the motivation of a man's acts from within the man. He alone is both outside and inside the human will. He alone can comprehend the interrelation of temptation and guilt. Therefore God comprehends the origin of guilt more deeply than the guilty man himself. He recognizes the character of sin, for guilt takes on this character only in the eyes of God. Sin is always a sin against God, never against a human being or a human institution. God alone can forgive sin. The mystery of God is involved in the mystery of redemption. As the peace of God surpasses all understanding, so also does the forgiving love of God in Christ.

No man can forgive the sin of his fellow man. Here ends the analogy between the human and the divine act of forgiveness. It is precisely this infinite distance between God and man which enables Christ to establish an infinite nearness between God and the contrite soul. In Christ the Supreme Judge gives up his majesty and deigns to become our friend. God alone can measure our sins. He alone can mitigate our remorse. He alone can acquit and redeem us, because we are infinitely indebted to him, and yet we cannot add the slightest contribution to his glory and power.

XI

Personal and Collective Guilt

And the Lord God called unto Adam, and said unto him, Where art thou? And he said, I heard thy voice in the garden, and I was afraid, because I was naked; and I hid myself. And he said, Who told thee that thou wast naked? Hast thou eaten of the tree, whereof I commanded thee that thou shouldest not eat? And the man said, The woman whom thou gavest to be with me, she gave me of the tree, and I did eat. And the Lord God said unto the woman, What is this that thou hast done? And the woman said, The serpent beguiled me, and I did eat. And the Lord God said unto the serpent, Because thou hast done this, thou art cursed above all cattle, and above every beast of the field; upon thy belly shalt thou go, and dust shalt thou eat all the days of thy life: And I will put enmity between thee and the woman, and between thy seed and her seed; it shall bruise thy head, and thou shalt bruise his heel. Unto the woman he said, I will greatly multiply thy sorrow and thy conception; in sorrow thou shalt bring forth children; and thy desire shall be to thy husband, and he shall rule over thee. And unto Adam he said, Because thou hast hearkened unto the voice of thy wife, and hast eaten of the tree, of which I commanded thee, saying, Thou shalt not eat of it: cursed is the ground for thy sake; in sorrow shalt thou eat of it all the days of thy life; Thorns also and thistles shall it bring forth to thee; and thou shalt eat the herb of the field; In the sweat of thy face shalt thou eat bread, till thou return unto the ground; for out of it wast thou taken: for dust thou art, and unto dust shalt thou return.

—Genesis 3:9-19

The story of the fall, each time we read it, arouses divergent feelings in us. On the one hand, it appeals to common sense. Nothing is more obvious than the fact that all men are morally frail and fallible like Adam and Eve, and that the whole human race is contaminated by this "radical evil," as Kant calls it. On the other hand, we struggle against the idea that the voluntary transgression of two individuals, supposed to be the ancestors of all men, should have brought a verdict of guilty upon the whole human race—a verdict imposed in advance upon every individual—a verdict that no one can avoid however pure and noble his intentions may be.

These contrasting reactions seem to be provoked by antagonistic views implied in the story itself. According to one interpretation, which we may call imaginative, Adam and Eve are a pair of blessed lovers living under the spell of complete harmony with each other and with God their Creator, enjoying thus the highest happiness imaginable. This view, presented in all its fullness and fascination in the graphic description of Milton, furthermore depicts the peculiar and unique circumstances which ultimately lead to the destruction of the happy scene and to the radical deterioration of their life. This deterioration is the result of transgressing a particular commandment given to them as two individuals and to them alone. According to the other interpretation, which we may call the speculative or doctrinal, the story offers an explanation of the origin of evil. In this view, Adam and Eve are not only a certain man and a certain woman, but also representations of every man and every woman, personified concepts as it were of generic man. It is characteristic that the Hebrew word *Adam* signifies both the name of the first man and man in general.

The imaginative view stresses the principle of individual responsibility and guilt; the speculative view, on the contrary, emphasizes the generic root of man's sinfulness. One illustrates the unrestricted freedom of choice in Adam and Eve as individual moral persons; the other enjoins a restriction on the free will of every mortal person. Eve's decision is influenced by the persuasive voice of the tempting serpent, but this feature in the imaginative view of the story only stresses the fact that Eve and Adam fail to resist temptation, that both succumb. They are by no means bound to act as they do. The speculative view, on the other hand, suggests that the action of the first human couple predetermines the scope of freedom of all actions of man in general. All descendants of Adam and Eve have to succumb to temptations of some analogous kind. The original sin illustrates the fact that each man belongs to an all-embracing community of sinners from which no one can deliberately and voluntarily withdraw. Adam and Eve are only the first members of that community.

Moral individualism and moral collectivism thus are in conflict. They clash with each other. The attempt to reconcile these antagonistic perspectives in a system of thought, however deeply conceived and however sagaciously carried through, ultimately breaks down. Reason confronts an insoluble contradiction. The two views can be related to two historical interpretations of guilt. Greek tragedy tends toward the collectivistic trend by tracing back individual transgressions to the operation of an inescapable fate; Shakespearean tragedy emphasizes the origin of evil in the personal will of the individual agent. Modern man has shown a growing distaste for the collectivistic aspect in the story of the fall as expressed in the dogma of original sin, and has adopted the individualistic element alone. Rousseau even went so far as to assert that the original goodness of man has never been lost; it has only been impaired by an unnatural form of civilization and society, and it can and should be recovered by an appropriate system of education.

For us today the idea of collective guilt has assumed a new significance in connection with the question of the guilt of the German nation. Is the nation as such to be arraigned? Or are only the leaders responsible for the sufferings inflicted upon millions by their decisions? German churchmen like Pastor Niemoeller have made confessions in public that amounted to a self-accusation on the part of the entire German nation. In Germany a discussion has ensued about the right and wrong of such confessions, and the opinion has been voiced that collective responsibility is a morally absurd postulate, that only those Germans who voluntarily and actively participated in the Nazi crimes can be called into account. The head of the religious wing of the German existentialists, Karl Jaspers, rejected with the strongest reasons the idea of a collective guilt. He insisted that the individual alone possesses a moral conscience, and that the individual has no responsibility for actions perpetrated by other persons. Jaspers argues that collective guilt could only be established if it could be proved that every German citizen voluntarily and actively supported the Nazi government. This is far from being the case. One has only to remember that countless Germans abhorred Nazism in its ideology as well as in its practices, and that they were coerced by the superior material force of official Germany to fight for Hitler's cause. Morally, they are each therefore as innocent and unimpeachable as any citizen of the victorious nations.

It cannot be denied that Jaspers' reasons are very strong and even irrefutable from the strictly moral point of view; that is, as long as it is held that men are not morally obliged to become martyrs. The very essence of martyrdom transcends the moral consciousness and points to the religious sphere. Man cannot be bound by moral obligation to lay down his life until he believes that such a sacrifice agrees with and is required by the will of God. The extreme position of the German who hated Hitler and his system but was coerced to obey the dictator's commands only illuminates like a sudden flash of lightning the real human scene. It discloses the limits of the sovereignty and freedom of man as an individual moral person.

The individual person confronts an alternative: he can either submit to the order of society in which he lives— an order which in the last analysis is never completely sinless, an order which is an all-embracing community of sinners, an order to which he intrinsically belongs—or he must be prepared and willing to suffer martyrdom. As long as a man sticks to his idea of an absolutely autonomous conscience, he is not absolutely free; rather he gains absolute freedom only when he surrenders himself to the will of God. God may require the supreme sacrifice of him at any moment. Man is much more entangled in the mesh of human relationships than he would like to think. He is much less autonomous than he has been painted in modern times. As a moral person, he is much less isolated than the idea of moral responsibility would suppose. This insight is on the one hand humiliating; it infringes upon the idea of man's moral dignity so dear to the founders of the modern spirit of the Renaissance. But on the other hand it opens the avenue to a much greater and deeper freedom, because it frees man from the burden of a responsibility which he is not strong enough to bear alone. He can uphold his moral dignity only when he admits that he belongs to the community of sinners, and that therefore he is unable to sustain his moral dignity out of his own resources. By humiliating himself he is exalted; by exalting himself he is humiliated. This is the Christian wisdom.

This wisdom rests ultimately on the collectivistic theme within the story of the fall. The spiritual excellence of the story unites and conciliates the opposites, individualism and collectivism, but its greatest excellence is that it subordinates man's individual freedom to man's destiny, which transcends this freedom. Only thus can the community of sinners be transformed into the community of the redeemed. The very possibility of redemption and salvation derives from the tragic fatality of sin. If the individual could carry the burden of responsibility himself, he would never be impelled to seek and to accept forgiveness. The autonomous conscience must finally revert into self-righteousness, and the self-righteous individual must finally reject the grace and mercy of Christ.

XII

The Mystery of Charity

Though I speak with the tongues of men and of angels, and have not charity, I am become as sounding brass, or a tinkling cymbal. And though I have the gift of prophecy, and understand all mysteries, and all knowledge; and though I have all faith, so that I could remove mountains, and have not charity, I am nothing. And though I bestow all my goods to feed the poor, and though I give my body to be burned, and have not charity, it profiteth me nothing. Charity suffereth long, and is kind; charity envieth not; charity vaunteth not itself, is not puffed up, Doth not behave itself unseemly, seeketh not her own, is not easily provoked, thinketh no evil; Rejoiceth not in iniquity, but rejoiceth in the truth; Beareth all things, believeth all things, hopeth all things, endureth all things. Charity never faileth: but whether there be prophecies, they shall fail; whether there be tongues, they shall cease; whether there be knowledge, it shall vanish away. For we know in part, and we prophesy in part. But when that which is perfect is come, then that which is in part shall be done away. When I was a child, I spake as a child, I understood as a child, I thought as a child: but when I became a man, I put away childish things. For now we see through a glass, darkly; but then face to face: now I know in part; but then shall I know even as also I am known. And now abideth faith, hope, charity, these three; but the greatest of these is charity.

—I Cor. 13

This song of songs praising the supreme and unique excellence of charity or spiritual love is so persuasive and enchanting that we may easily overlook the serious problems it implies. Who would not accept the wonderful message that love surpasses all other attitudes or activities of the human soul? —that where love reigns everything else fades into nothingness? —that love is more sublime than knowledge, more powerful than prophecy, more significant than even faith and hope when these are not animated and inspired by love? —that nothing could ever be a substitute for love, not the highest virtue, not the deepest wisdom, not all the riches of philosophical or theological profundity? —that no sagacity, no acuteness of the thinking mind can ever reach ultimate truth, if love is absent, if love does not direct and govern our hearts?

This persuasive and appealing message is by no means simple and self-evident. For Paul not only exalts charity above everything else in an almost ecstatic fashion, but he also goes so far as to disparage everything else. It is especially striking that he decries so emphatically the value of gnosis as contrasted with agape. "Charity never fails . . . whether there be knowledge, it shall vanish away, for we know in part . . . but when that which is perfect is come, then that which is in part shall be done away." Here Paul bluntly states that knowledge by its very na-

*Published as "A Meditation on I Cor. XIII" in *Anglican Theological Review*, XXX, No. 4 (October, 1948), 216-18.

ture is imperfect, fragmentary, and therefore unfit to arrive at its goal: ultimate truth. Not gnosis, but the *unio mystica* achieved by spiritual love fulfills the highest desire of knowledge itself.

Paul uses a simile to illustrate this relation between the imperfect and the perfect. Knowledge belongs to the childish things which the mature man puts away. It is only the immature mind which may be convinced that ultimate truth can be reached by knowledge. The adult no longer indulges in that error. He is convinced that love alone can penetrate into the heart of God. When love performs this mystery, the childish pride of the thinking mind is overcome.

The history of Christian thought demonstrates the tremendous influence of this mystical doctrine of Paul's. It also demonstrates that this influence was not always strong enough to prevent theologians and philosophers from disregarding the warning imminent in the ecstatic praise of charity. Paul seems to have foreseen that Greek speculation would turn out to be a most dangerous rival of the Christian message; he thus invalidated it in advance. Of course, it is no small task for the thinking mind to practice what Paul prescribed and to renounce its own capacity. Only in a mature state of development does philosophy disclaim its ability to produce a knowledge of ultimate truth—a knowledge of the nature of God.

Ever anew we have to learn to comprehend the wisdom of Paul in this respect. Ever again the thinking mind has to bow down before the man in whose heart divine charity lives and operates, before the childlike believer in the love of God who is more mature than the childish believer in scientific or speculative truth.

There is another aspect of Paul's mystical exaltation of spiritual love, an aspect perhaps even more striking than the first one. Paul not only disparages knowledge, with prophecy, as a lower and imperfect stage of man's spiritual development, but he also calls faith and hope less than charity. "Though I have all faith, so that I could remove mountains, and have not charity, I am nothing." Agape not only consummates and fulfills prophecy and gnosis, but it also makes faith and hope perfect; nay, it replaces them, because it contains them in itself. Charity "beareth all things, *believeth* all things, *hopeth* all things." Faith and hope are intrinsic constituents of that love which Paul praises, and without that love, faith and hope are empty and vain. Why does love in the sense of the Pauline mystical hymn excel faith and hope? Or, to put it differently, in what respect are faith and hope deficient and insignificant, or at least incomplete, without love? This question is the more serious, when we reflect how central to dogma is the term faith.

Is not faith the sum total of Christianity, or at least the basis and the zenith of its total structure? How can it be surpassed by anything else, even by love? Does Paul think of *pistis* [faith] here as a merely theoretical assent to true propositions, as Cardinal Newman defines the nature of faith? Does he rank love higher than faith because, rather than a theoretical attitude, it is the very practice and living confirmation of faith? Does he exalt love precisely because he thinks more highly of practice than of theory? Does he assume that faith is more akin to knowledge and therefore less perfect than love?

Paul declares that faith sees the truth "through a glass, darkly"—in a mirror, not directly, not as the truth is in itself; faith is therefore as incomplete, as fragmentary as knowledge, however great the difference between the two attitudes may otherwise be. Faith appears in this rapturous vision of love as imperfect, because it cannot bring about the mystical union with God any more than knowledge can. Love alone succeeds in fulfilling the ultimate longing of the human heart. The lover alone is intimately and closely at one with the beloved; love alone accomplishes the miracle of bridging the gap that separates man and God, as it also unifies mankind with one another. Love alone sees face to face; that is to say, it has the power to traverse the infinite distance which divides the sphere of sinful man from the abode of the holy and merciful God. In and through love the "divine-human encounter" is completed and made absolute. This seems to be the reason why Paul says that faith as much as knowledge and prophecy is surpassed by charity.

The same is even more true with respect to hope. The man who merely hopes is even farther from possessing the object of his hope than the believer. As long as he hopes, he cannot be entirely free from fear. And as John says (I John 4:18), "There is no fear in love; but perfect love casteth out fear . . . he that feareth is not made perfect in love." The same can be said of him who hopes; he is not yet made perfect in love. Love by its very nature fulfills the desire of hope. When love prevails, hope is outshone and surpassed. Uncertainty and imperfection are replaced by the certainty and perfect joy of possession.

Thus the superiority of charity may be set forth. Of course, in the theology of Paul taken as a whole, the three modes of spiritual life are inseparable. They represent three perspectives on the same basic attitude, namely, man's response to the grace of Christ; sometimes they are summed up under the title of faith, sometimes under that of charity. Is it surprising, after all, that the great apostle of Jesus Christ should have sung the ecstatic hymn of love? Biblical faith from the outset and throughout its development is grounded in love as the ultimate bond between God and man. *One* line stretches from the commandment, "Thou shalt love the Lord thy God with all thy heart, and with all thy soul and with all thy mind," to the final simple yet majestic definition, "God is love." Seen in this perspective, chapter 13 of the first epistle to the Corinthians represents the summit of the Christian message, as it also provides the best foundation for a sound Christian theology.

XIII

The Tabernacle of God

And the disciples of John and of the Pharisees used to fast: and they come and say unto him, Why do the disciples of John and of the Pharisees fast, but thy disciples fast not? And Jesus said unto them, Can the children of the bridechamber fast, while the bridegroom is with them? as long as they have the bridegroom with them, they cannot fast. But the days will come, when the bridegroom shall be taken away from them, and then shall they fast in those days. No man also seweth a piece of new cloth on an old garment: else the new piece that filled it up taketh away from the old, and the rent is made worse. And no man putteth new wine into old bottles: else the new wine doth burst the bottles, and the wine is spilled, and the bottles will be marred: but new wine must be put into new bottles.

—Mark 2:18-22

What is the essence of the new cloth and the new wine to which Jesus refers? To discuss the difference between the Old and New Testaments in a short address would be foolish, but it may be permissible to venture a short answer, stressing one point of difference which might be of some significance for us today.

Often we hear that the incarnation is the center of the Christian religion and that the good news is the appearance of God himself in the figure of a man on the scene of human history. In Jesus Christ the Logos becomes flesh; the Infinite descends from his throne; the Creator of heaven and earth assumes the humble frame of a finite man; the eternal enters time. This, it is said, is the core of the Christian message, and the foundation of the Christian church is an outcome of this unique event. In the midst of secular and transitory institutions, Jesus initiates a holy community, a divine kingdom, of historical actuality and power and yet not of this world.

The incarnation certainly is of central significance. The unique and revolutionary message of the gospel, however, is not precisely circumscribed as long as it is seen in the interpenetration of the eternal and the temporal, or in the appearance of God within the setting of human history. It is the peculiar character of biblical revelation throughout the Old Testament to merge these diametric opposites. The Creator is also and primarily the lord of history; history is his revelation, the scene on which he acts. Crea-

tion itself as depicted in Genesis is both a divine decree
and a historical event. Is this identity any less a miracle
than the incarnation? Although in the Old Testament
revelation, God does not send his son, he does appear to
Moses and he does elect his prophets, in whose hearts and
in whose words he is present and through whose mouths
he himself speaks. Moreover, in choosing a particular, historical nation as his special servant and people, God allies
himself with finite humanity and takes a part in the
historic destiny of mankind.

The novel element in the New Testament is not the
intrinsic unity of the eternal and the temporal, but the
culmination and consummation of this alliance in Jesus
the Christ. He is not one of the prophets, but the Son
of God; the interpenetration of the divine and the human, of the transcendent and the immanent, reaches its
zenith in him. He is the consummation and the end of
biblical history; he opens a period in which past and future no longer are of the highest spiritual significance.
They bow down instead to the presence of the Eternal.

The church represents the community of those whose
inner life is no longer bound up with the hopes and fears
of a secular though holy nation; rather it stands in the
world only as a witness that God transcends the world,
and that man also has to transcend the world in order to
participate in the holiness of Christ. The church is basically not a historical but an eschatological body. The center of Christianity is not the incarnation but the cross and
the resurrection. In the Old Testament, God descends
from on high. This movement of the Eternal toward the

temporal begins with the creation. In the Logos Incarnate this movement comes to its ultimate and definitive end, and a new movement sets in, from the finite toward the infinite, from the world back to God.

This new movement has a momentous consequence. The Old Testament is concerned with the way God reveals himself to a particular nation. God is the king of that nation; the messiah expected by that nation will be a new David. Throughout the Old Testament, God speaks, not to the individual soul, but to his people. In the New Testament this order is radically reversed. Jesus is the Christ, not as a new prophet in Israel, but as himself: a unique, individual personality. His disciples also are elected as individuals, and the apostles are individually called upon to preach and to baptize men as men, as beings endowed each with a human soul, not as members of a historical community. This is the new wine, the new cloth, that cannot be adapted to the old.

The new community consists of single individuals united exclusively in Christ; it consists of souls in a direct, living relationship to the holy God. Jesus, therefore, stressed strongly and in a new fashion the contrast between world and soul, between appearance and reality, between the outer and the inner conduct. "What shall it profit a man, if he shall gain the whole world, and lose his own soul?" This was a message which had not been heard before. Jesus addressed himself to men who had been released from the bonds of history, to men as men.

As the creation is the first historical act of God, so the incarnation is his last. Since that event we know that

God is first of all the God of the individual human soul, and only because he is this is he also the lord of history who guides and judges the nations. The Old Testament order is transformed into its opposite. Through Jesus the unity between the political and the spiritual body, between the secular frame of history and the eternal word of God is no longer what it had been before him. "Render unto Caesar the things which be Caesar's, and unto God the things which be God's." Consequently, the idea of the Messiah is also transformed. He is no longer conceived of as a national hero who will bring about Israel's final triumph, but as the shepherd of souls who conquers all nationalism. The cross testifies to this victory of the Spirit over the power of nations, and thereby completes biblical history.

From now on faith is not bound up with the destiny of a historical nation. Although history in the secular sense is not deprived of spiritual and prophetic dimensions, these dimensions are not the primary concern of faith. Secular history is subject to prophetic interpretation not directly but only indirectly, inasmuch as individual souls are involved actively and passively in the processes of national and political change. The center of spiritual life has shifted from the state to the individual, from the world to the soul, from outward events to the inner destiny, from the kingdom of nations to the kingdom of God. The Father of Jesus is not first the lord of history and second the savior of sinful man, but rather he is first the Savior and only as such is he the lord of history.

The new, the heavenly, Jerusalem is no locality on

earth. God is Spirit. The exceptional mission of a single historical people has been surpassed. The people of God comprises all men: "And I heard a great voice out of heaven saying, Behold, the tabernacle of God is with men, and he will dwell with them, and they shall be his people, and God himself shall be with them, and be their God" (Revelation 21:3).

XIV

Holy Authority

And when he was come into the temple, the chief priests and the elders of the people came unto him as he was teaching, and said, By what authority doest thou these things? and who gave thee this authority? And Jesus answered and said unto them, I also will ask you one thing, which if ye tell me, I in like wise will tell you by what authority I do these things. The baptism of John, whence was it? from heaven, or of men? And they reasoned with themselves, saying, If we shall say, From heaven; he will say unto us, Why did ye not then believe him? But if we shall say, Of men; we fear the people; for all hold John as a prophet. And they answered Jesus, and said, We cannot tell. And he said unto them, Neither tell I you by what authority I do these things.

—Matt. 21:23-27

"By what authority doest thou these things? and who gave thee this authority?" This question is not confined to the person of Jesus, but can equally be raised with respect to the great figures of the Old Testament, and with respect to the disciples and apostles who acknowledged the authority of Jesus. The same question may be repeated each time a leader of the Christian church or a Christian theologian makes a momentous decision in which practical conflicts or dogmatic issues are concerned. Certainly, the degree of authority in such decisions depends upon the degree to which any innovations reform the life and thought of the spirit. The deeper they cut into traditional habits of thought and faith, the more vividly and anxiously will the question be put: "By what authority doest thou these things? and who gave thee this authority?" Jesus himself says in the story that every man who has faith and does not doubt can perform the same things he does. Firm faith can remove mountains. Authority is given to them whose faith is unshakable and unconditional.

The question raised, however, is not fully answered by this hint. The authority of Christ is derived from God himself; it has a divine source, but the authority of men cannot be secured and acknowledged on the same basis. And yet, such authority has been needed from the beginning of the Christian church through every phase of its history, in every decision that has been made, at every stage in the development of dogma and doctrine, of administrative and liturgical practices—this authority is never at the end of its unfolding activity as long as the church is alive, as long as we live in an ever changing world which demands new decisions and the solution of new problems.

The Reformation, which did away with many of the habits of faith and practice developed in the church for centuries, officially sanctioned and even sanctified the formidable question: "By what authority doest thou these things?" Up to the Reformation, Christendom could believe in continuing divine guidance because the pope was regarded as the vicar of Christ himself. But this assurance suddenly was destroyed. The authority of the pope, of the councils, and of the entire visible church living on earth which had handed down so many solemn and great decisions of the past was spurned in a way comparable to the revolution that Jesus initiated. This was of course not on the same level of spiritual significance and power. The Reformers pointed to the Bible as the supreme and ultimate source of authority.

Once the Bible seemed indisputably clear. This surety no longer exists. Today we know that the Bible is in some respects a human book; at the same time we believe that it is the medium for the word of God. The letter needs spiritual interpretation and intellectual criticism. Thus the question arises with unabated, nay even with strongly increased intensity, "By what authority doest thou these things?" By what authority do we interpret the letter, by what authority do we claim truth for dogmatic pronouncements, for our conceptions concerning the office of the church or its relations to the state, and so on.

At a recent meeting of Protestant theologians who were discussing fundamental problems, the need of an unimpeachable criterion of truth was expressed with an almost desperate urgency, aroused by the seemingly hopeless variety of diverging and contradictory viewpoints. One of the scholars pointed with a scarcely concealed envy to the Roman Catholic church which is so much better protected against the danger of a complete disintegration generated by profound and irreparable disagreements. But what genuinely Protestant Christian would be willing for the sake of unity and unanimity to pay the price exacted by the system of Roman authority? The conviction that the freedom of conscience is a divine gift was the dynamic force in the whole movement of the Reformation, and it cannot be sacrificed even in order to safeguard the Protestant community against the threat of dissolution and self-destruction. It was the Roman kind of authority which Jesus repudiated.

No easy solution can be advanced to avoid the tremendous difficulties of seeking an ultimate criterion of truth. In smaller matters like those of the natural sciences it is possible to establish exact measurements, but in the realm of theological and spiritual truth not only is such a measurement impossible, but it is foolish and pretentious to demand it or to hope for it. "The wind bloweth where it listeth, and thou hearest the sound thereof, but canst not tell whence it cometh, and whither it goeth: so is every one that is born of the Spirit" (John

3:8). The lack of any human tribunal, any visible or tangible authority, is the glory and the criterion of divine power. And yet we human beings, living on earth and under finite conditions, cannot receive the divine truth without conjoining it with symbols or signs and without demanding authority for them as the shell that contains the pearl of great price. We cannot avoid the contradiction that lies in claiming truth for our own spiritual convictions when we know they are conditioned by time and space—by historical and individual circumstances which make them finite and relative.

In the last analysis the same contradiction is the paradox of the incarnation. This paradox is repeated each time the church or the individual makes a decision to stand for convictions, to introduce innovations, or to defend dogmatic or theological statements. The authority behind all these actions is ultimately God himself. No direct, official, visible criterion can be applied to distinguish the right from the wrong claim, the true from the false prophet. Since the Reformation we have been aware that the Christian church can err, and that no principle of infallibility can enforce our fidelity or vindicate our decisions. Although the eternal salvation of the community and of the individual depends upon the question of authority, no court can assure us of a right response. The church is not, as the Roman tradition would have it, a spiritual life insurance company. No such company exists; indeed, the very idea of one contradicts the character of the spiritual life as much as it contradicts the holiness of the Holy Spirit.

It is amazing that in spite of the utter fallibility of men God finds the means to uphold his authority through the medium of such frail and feeble instruments as we are. He recovers and re-establishes this authority again and again when false prophets have prevailed. That God possesses this power makes life meaningful; the belief in this power is the fundamental condition for a meaningful life. It is this belief which solves all the contradictions of life. In the end the hint given by Jesus in the text is the key to the problem of authority: faith and faith alone is its source; faith and faith alone, unshakable and unconditional, can encourage us to trust a holy authority in the midst of unholy conditions and through all the relativities and contingencies of history.

XV

Discipleship and the Cross

Where is the wise? where is the scribe? where is the disputer of this world? hath not God made foolish the wisdom of this world? For after that in the wisdom of God the world by wisdom knew not God, it pleased God by the foolishness of preaching to save them that believe. For the Jews require a sign, and the Greeks seek after wisdom: But we preach Christ crucified, unto the Jews a stumblingblock, and unto the Greeks foolishness; But unto them which are called, both Jews and Greeks, Christ the power of God, and the wisdom of God.

—I Cor. 1:20-24

"We preach Christ crucified." It is not easy to imagine how this message was received by the contemporaries of Paul. It is easy, of course, to understand that the majority of Jews and of Greeks who heard him speak were indignant and rejected the new faith simply because they did not grasp its meaning. How could the Jews accept the idea of a messiah who was not victorious but had died in the most ignominious way? Such a messiah certainly did not agree with their ancient expectations and hopes. To them the message seemed a mockery of their cherished convictions. It is no wonder that they stumbled over such a perverse interpretation. The Greeks, especially the cultivated among them, were completely unable to comprehend that a crucified man, whatever he might have said or done, should be regarded as the savior of all mankind. Their notions of wisdom and of divine power contrasted strongly with such a message; they could not help calling it foolish and dismissing the preacher as an ignorant and superstitious babbler.

It is not easy to imagine how the ancient believer could overcome these prejudices which obstructed the acceptance of the new message. This message was not only in disagreement with the traditions both of Jew and of Greek, but in disagreement with common sense and natural feelings. It was so paradoxical that all men had to take offense at it. That it was nevertheless believed by some, and that it finally conquered the minds and souls

103

of the nations, is a miracle. The word paradoxical literally means "against the opinion." To believe that a person crucified represents the highest power and the deepest wisdom of God is certainly against the opinion of natural man. Such a message contradicted, and still contradicts, all common conceptions of power and wisdom, be they of Jewish or of Greek origin. It is still paradoxical today and has not lost its challenging and appalling character. The natural man still stumbles over its content, and is inclined to reject it as foolish. How can the power of God manifest itself in the image of agony and utter helplessness? How can the wisdom of God be revealed by an event which demonstrates the complete failure of a man's life? These questions are indeed embarrassing and provoking, and should not be disregarded merely because the Christian faith has succeeded in convincing the nations. Every century has stumbled anew over the meaning of the cross and has labored to interpret it in ever new forms on ever new levels of understanding.

The cross is challenging because it implies a deep and irreconcilable opposition between the world in which we live and strive and work and the divine Creator who made the world and who made us so that we might live and work and strive for its improvement and for our happiness. The cross seems to contradict the basic condition of our life and of all endeavor and toil. The cross seems to cut the tie between world and God so radically and so unconditionally as to make all attempts at the improvement of our condition and of ourselves vain and meaningless.

That the greatest love on earth is answered by the greatest cruelty—that the most sublime wisdom is treated with absolute contempt and ends in the most horrible catastrophe—implies an implacable revolt of man against the divine when it appears in the midst of established institutions and traditions. This suggests that man is so thoroughly blind and deaf to the grace and love of God as to be incurable. It is no wonder that natural man tries to protect himself against such a truth, that he instinctively defends his natural aspirations and inclinations against the devastating effect of this most gloomy, most tragic revelation.

The serious and repulsive meaning of the cross is often eclipsed by the resurrection; all the more so, because the crucifixion seems to belong to the past, whereas the resurrection has ushered in the eternal reign and glory of the Lord. The cross does have a lasting significance as long as time goes on and man lives in history. The opposition between our world and the divine is not overcome by the eternal Christ who sits on the right hand of God. It is real, and will remain real until the second advent, when the Lord will come again with power and great glory.

The cross is an enduring warning that the believer in Christ may encounter at any time the same abysmal hate and the same furious persecution which Christ himself confronted. It is a warning that the Christian believer should never expect a truce with the world. In our days the warning has taken on renewed significance and gravity, since a new hostility toward Christ has come to life and come into power in many European countries. This hostility has sharpened the opposition between world and God and has generated a new type of martyrdom.

In our days the cross means the visible sign of that ultimate courage demanded from all who dare to resist the antichrist. One of the most courageous and most loyal disciples to pay the full cost of discipleship was Dietrich Bonhoeffer, who was for some time a student in this seminary. His writings, including *The Cost of Discipleship,*[*] illustrate the new spirit of martyrdom as it has arisen in our sad epoch. Let me quote a number of passages which illustrate this spirit:

> When we know the cross, we are no longer afraid of the truth.
> The only man who has the right to say that he is justified by grace alone, is the man who has left all to follow Christ.
> When Christ calls a man, He bids him come and die.
> The Christian is committed to a daily warfare against the world. Every day he encounters new temptations, and every day he must suffer anew for Jesus Christ's sake.
> If we refuse to take up our cross and submit to suffering and rejection at the hands of men, we forfeit our fellowship with Christ . . .
> The community which is the subject of the beatitudes is the community of the crucified. With him it has lost all, and with him it has found all.

Bonhoeffer was aware that the cross is not only a warning, but also a consolation. As sufferers for the sake of

---

[*]Trans. R. H. Fuller (New York: Macmillan, 1949). Quoted by permission.

Christ we shall enjoy his fellowship and feel it as a token of grace and a privilege. Those, Bonhoeffer says, "who live in communion with Him cannot really suffer . . . Jesus overcomes suffering by means of suffering."

Only a very few, only the elect, will attain to the lofty height at which the German martyr arrived in the hard and bitter school of Hitler's regime. For the rest of us the word of Luther, which Bonhoeffer quotes, holds good: "Bewilderment is the true comprehension."

XVI

Letter and Spirit

Do we begin again to commend ourselves? or need we, as some others, epistles of commendation to you, or letters of commendation from you? Ye are our epistle written in our hearts, known and read of all men: Forasmuch as ye are manifestly declared to be the epistle of Christ ministered by us, written not with ink, but with the Spirit of the living God; not in tables of stone, but in fleshly tables of the heart. And such trust have we through Christ to God-ward: Not that we are sufficient of ourselves to think anything as of ourselves; but our sufficiency is of God; Who also hath made us able ministers of the new testament; not of the letter, but of the spirit: for the letter killeth, but the spirit giveth life. But if the ministration of death, written and engraven in stones, was glorious, so that the children of Israel could not stedfastly behold the face of Moses for the glory of his countenance; which glory was to be done away; How shall not the ministration of the spirit be rather glorious? For if the ministration of condemnation be glory, much more doth the ministration of righteousness exceed in glory.

—II Cor. 3:1-9

The antagonism between letter and spirit is so familiar to us that we easily overlook the difficulties involved in the distinction and the problems ensuing from it. Usually we take it for granted that the antagonism lies between the literal, original, primary meaning of a word or a phrase, and its spiritual, figurative, or metaphorical meaning—a distinction first emphasized by Origen, who made it a principle of biblical exegesis. This contrast is certainly not in the foreground of Paul's discussion, if it is intimated at all. Since Paul's language is metaphorical throughout, and moreover rapidly changes the meaning of terms, some effort must be exerted to discover the central meaning of his distinction between letter and spirit.

The opposition between an original and a figurative meaning is not Paul's point of departure. In comparing the Corinthian Christians with his written epistles, the apostle is contrasting the living spirit of human beings with the deadness of the material, physical letters. Behind this comparison looms another, which soon comes to the fore: the epistles are after all not just dead, material letters, but spiritual messengers carrying the living mind of Paul himself to the believers. There is a spirit alive in the letters, a spirit which is supposed to bring life to the members of the Christian community. The deeper contrast between the epistles and the Christians is therefore not that between the dead letters and the living souls, but that between the human spirit of Paul imparted in his epistles

111

to the Corinthians and the divine Spirit which has inscribed itself without any medium of words in the hearts of those who dedicate their lives to God.

This comparison is soon succeeded by a third which contrasts the tablets of Moses, on which God had engraved the words of his commandments, to the Christians, whose hearts God has directly impressed with his spirit; the tablets of stone are transformed into tablets of the heart. Here again it is not only the distinction between material carvings and spiritual meanings which represents the contrast of letter and spirit, but also the deeper and itself spiritual antagonism between the law of Moses and the New Testament. The law takes on the character of the letter, not merely because it is written on tablets of stone, but especially because it demands a literal obedience. The new meaning, on the contrary, conveys the unwritten spirit of the Lord, liberating the mind from slavish obedience to the letter, for "where the spirit of the Lord reigns, there is liberty." This interpretation is stressed by the confrontation of the two ministries: that of the old covenant, which was a ministry of condemnation and death because the letter kills, and that of the new covenant, which is a ministration of the spirit and therefore gives life and grants righteousness.

By this series of rapidly changing metaphors Paul arrives at an antagonism which is no longer concerned with the opposition between letter as being material and spirit as the source and recipient of immaterial meanings and immaterial life. Rather the opposition now lies between two kinds of message which differ from each other in *spirit.* Or to put it another way: the terms, letter and spirit, are themselves no longer used literally but spiritually, if we understand by "literal" the primary and familiar meaning of a word and by "spiritual" a figurative or metaphorical meaning.

Paul distinguishes letter and spirit neither in the exegetical sense of different strata of meanings nor in the sense of two different strata of existence, material and immaterial. He is, rather, mainly interested in distinguishing different stages in the development of faith in the revelation of God, that is, two kinds of loyalty to God, and two ways God has dealt with man. He wants to glorify the new spirit of Christ, which no longer enslaves men under the yoke of a law they cannot obey but in which rather Christ accepts them out of his infinite mercy and love, and thereby overcomes the tyranny of the letter. Paul wants to make it clear that the spirit of the law, which is the spirit of the letter, is surpassed by the spirit of love, which is the spirit of God. In the last analysis his opposition of letter and spirit coincides with the antagonism between a moralistic and a redemptive conception of the ultimate purpose of God.

Is there no relation whatever between this Pauline interpretation of the terms letter and spirit and their methodical application as introduced by the great theologian of the early church, Origen? Such a relation does exist, although Paul does not directly speak about it. After all, the distinction of strata or stages in the development of revelation and faith has this in common with the distinction of strata or stages in the realm of meaning. In both cases an order of rank is established between higher and lower conceptions of a single subject—according to Paul, the spirit of God, and according to Origen and his successors, the spirit of the Bible as the word of God. Paul insists that in the Old Testament God has not yet revealed himself in all his glory; Origen insists that there are two or three types of meaning throughout Scripture which differ from each other in the depth of meaning they reveal. To contrast the material and the immaterial spheres of reality is to contrast their values. This contrast of values is the common denominator of the Pauline and the traditional, methodical use of the terms letter and spirit. As the realm of material things is lower than that of the immaterial, and touches upon the sphere of the meaningless, so also obedience to the letter of the law is lower than the spiritual freedom of the Christian. And again, interpretation of the Bible on the level of literalism, or as we say today, of fundamentalism, is lower than spiritual interpretation which discovers the metaphorical or allegorical meaning of the Bible and in this sense its spiritual meaning.

This mediation between the Pauline and the familiar application of the terms letter and spirit vindicates itself the more if we reflect that the metaphorical interpretation of the Bible is a product of Christian exegesis, and that the higher meaning discovered in the words of the Bible refers to the development from the Old to the New Testament, or in the language of Paul, to the development from the letter to the spirit. The higher we climb in the order of the Bible's revelation, the more spiritual grows its content, and at the same time the more metaphorical its language becomes. The things of the spirit can be expressed only in a spiritual manner, that is, in a metaphorical or imaginative way; material things alone can be presented in a literal way, that is, in unimaginative language. Insofar as the legalistic spirit of the law sticks to the letter, it lacks that spiritual imagination which is the excellence of the higher revelation of the gospel.

The letter kills, but the spirit gives life. This word is as true with respect to the Pauline distinction between law and love as it is with respect to the traditional distinction between the literal and the metaphorical meaning of words and phrases. The material, the historical, the linguistic conditions are only the medium or veil through which the eternal Spirit shines. In this truth all conceptions of letter and spirit converge.

XVII

The Delicate
Balance of the Spirit

But now I go my way to him that sent me; and none of you asketh me, Whither goest thou? But because I have said these things unto you, sorrow hath filled your heart. Nevertheless I tell you the truth; It is expedient for you that I go away: for if I go not away, the Comforter will not come unto you; but if I depart, I will send him unto you. And when he is come, he will reprove the world of sin, and of righteousness, and of judgment: Of sin, because they believe not on me; Of righteousness, because I go to my Father, and ye see me no more; Of judgment, because the prince of this world is judged. I have yet many things to say unto you, but ye cannot bear them now. Howbeit when he, the Spirit of truth, is come, he will guide you into all truth: for he shall not speak of himself; but whatsoever he shall hear, that shall he speak: and he will shew you things to come.

—John 16:5-13

The figure of the Paraclete or the Comforter is surrounded by mystery. In one place he seems to be identical with the Savior; in another place, he will be sent by Jesus after his departure in order to finish the work of salvation by teaching the full truth. This miraculous figure has attracted the minds of many thinkers and occasioned diverse speculations and interpretations. In the early church, Tertullian and the Gnostics were among the first to exult at the image of a Comforter who would come to ransom man from the bondage of error and ignorance. In connection with the idea of the Paraclete that of a third testament arose, a testament more spiritual and therefore more adequate than Holy Scripture. Modern German poets like Lessing and German metaphysicians like Hegel announced this spiritual gospel, and Hegel interpreted it in terms of his own speculative system, which was supposed to reveal the full and undisguised truth of which Holy Scripture gives only a veiled, imaginative account. Only philosophy can, according to his doctrine, fulfill the promise of the Paraclete, because only philosophy is able to say outright what is the essence of all things. Only pure reason and pure thought can disclose what is merely intimated, but still hidden, in the words of our Lord spoken while he walked in the flesh.

Jesus, on the authority of this kind of interpretation, knew very well that he could not reveal the truth in its unrestricted fullness as long as he used a parabolic language. He promised the disciples, therefore, that the plain truth would be made known to them only after he had left the earth. "These things have I spoken unto you in proverbs: but the time cometh when I shall no more speak unto you in proverbs, but I shall shew you plainly of the Father" (John 16:25). These thinkers do not interpret the word "plainly" by teaching that Jesus or the spirit could express the ultimate truth in a simple and easy way; how could this be possible? If it had been possible, then Jesus himself could have done it directly and immediately. The word "plainly" can therefore be taken to mean that the Paraclete was no longer to speak in the imaginative, metaphorical or figurative language of Jesus, but instead would speak in gnostic or philosophical terms adequately fitted to the character of the undisguised, and in that sense plain, truth.

This interpretation is tempting indeed. It can explain why Jesus declared it was expedient for the disciples that he go away, and why he added that if he did not go away, the Comforter would not come. It is tempting to conclude that the sensible and fleshly existence of Jesus had to cease to let the invisible character of the truth come to the fore. It is tempting to vindicate in this way the high aspirations of speculative reason, and to lend plausibility to the claim that only philosophy can fulfill the offices of the Paraclete. Is the speculative thinker not right when he insists that the imaginative language of the parables conceals a meaning which is not merely imaginative but realistic or plain? And is he not also right when he maintains that this plain meaning is purely intellectual and therefore to be transmitted only by purely conceptual means? Is he not right when he discovers in this passage from John a Platonic trend of thought, a reminiscence of the Ideas or Forms which express the truth more plainly than do the parabolic narratives? Is it not correct to say that the alternative to imagination is pure reason or intellectual intuition as explicated by speculative philosophy?

The author of the Fourth Gospel no doubt had some knowledge of the Platonic realm of Ideas and was, at least to a certain degree, in sympathy with a philosophic conception of truth and knowledge. Does he not stress again and again the spiritual nature of things divine? Does he not solemnly proclaim that God is Spirit and that they who worship God must worship him in spirit and in truth? Does he not assure us through the mouth of Jesus that the Spirit will guide us into all truth? In the first epistle of John we even read: "The Spirit is truth" (I John 5:6). The conclusion drawn by Christian Platonists that the basic views of Greek idealism and the spiritually conceived gospel are at least in harmony (if not identical) seems very alluring indeed. At least the Johannine version of the gospel seems to support such a harmony.

One should not, however, underrate the chasm which separates even the most spiritual explanation of the Christian message from all philosophical understanding. Least of all should one disregard the momentous difference between spirit and reason; one should not forget that the very word truth has a different meaning in the gospel from its use in the context of science and thought to mean a theoretical agreement between our concepts and reality. In the gospel, truth is rather the truth of life which we can reach only by faith in the Giver of life and in the Redeemer of sin. For all his stress upon knowledge and truth, the author of the Fourth Gospel is not an intellectualist; he, like all biblical writers, has always the practical and redemptive meaning of the word truth in his mind. It is this meaning which he calls spiritual. Although he emphasizes the supersensible character of truth, he does not point thereby to pure thought in the sense that Plato does, but to the purity of the heart; he does not appeal to the energy of the searching and inquiring human intellect, but to the power of God operative in the human will; he wants to replace sensory imagination, not by logical and conceptual methods, but by that sublime vision which is inspired by the grace of Christ and the love of God. It is spiritual imagination he wishes to arouse in the soul of the believer, and which he says will prevail after Jesus has departed.

For the sake of this deeper devotion, of this more spiritual loyalty, Jesus declares it expedient that he disappear so that the eyes and ears may no longer divert the mind from grasping the spiritual nature of God and Christ. The Comforter whom he will send is not the speculative metaphysician. The truth the Paraclete is to disclose is not the truth of a philosophical system. The Spirit whom Jesus cites is not the spirit of a dialectical method, the spirit of the gnostics ancient and modern, but rather he is God himself who will come to judge the prince of this world. The world shall rejoice when Jesus passes away, because his death is the precondition of the coming of the kingdom of God—and not of speculative philosophy.

We must not exaggerate the gnostic aspect of the passage dealing with the Paraclete. We must not overlook the words which safeguard the interpretation against any philosophic exploitation. We must not overdo the Hellenic feature of the Fourth Gospel. After all, John is as mystical as is the whole Bible. Basically he agrees with Paul in his conceptions of spirit and truth, of knowledge and salvation. In both men we find that same delicate and perfect balance between elements which, separated from each other, lead either to metaphysical adventures or to gross superstition or—and this happens mostly—to a combination of the two. John as well as Paul avoids these dangers. It is this tender and yet powerful equilibrium which conquered the faith of the ancient world and which has survived so many speculative systems. Only if we stick to this perfect balance shall we penetrate the meaning of the Paraclete; only then will his edifying character be preserved.

XVIII

The Unknown God

Then Paul stood in the midst of Mars' hill, and said, Ye men of Athens, I perceive that in all things ye are too superstitious. For as I passed by, and beheld your devotions, I found an altar with the inscription, TO THE UNKNOWN GOD. Whom therefore ye ignorantly worship, him declare I unto you. God that made the world and all things therein, seeing that he is Lord of heaven and earth, dwelleth not in temples made with hands; Neither is worshipped with men's hands, as though he needed any thing, seeing he giveth to all life, and breath, and all things; And hath made of one blood all nations of men for to dwell on all the face of the earth, and hath determined the times before appointed, and the bounds of their habitation; That they should seek the Lord, if haply they might feel after him, and find him, though he be not far from every one of us: For in him we live, and move, and have our being; as certain also of your own poets have said, For we are also his offspring. Forasmuch then as we are the offspring of God, we ought not to think that the Godhead is like unto gold, or silver, or stone, graven by art and man's device. And the times of this ignorance God winked at; but now commandeth all men every where to repent: Because he hath appointed a day, in the which he will judge the world in righteousness by that man whom he hath ordained; whereof he hath given assurance unto all men, in that he hath raised him from the dead.

—Acts 17:22-31

When Paul went to Athens and addressed himself to the highly learned and sophisticated Greeks, a dramatic moment of the first order came about both in Paul's own career and in the history of the expansion of Christianity. Paul had met Greeks before and he had often attacked their superstitious adoration of their gods, but here in Athens he adapted his speech for the first time to the cultural standards of the highly cultivated group, and thus initiated that blend which was to dominate the church for many centuries. In fact one can call Paul, the author of that speech at Athens, a forerunner of Clement of Alexandria and his school. The two greatest movements in the history of mankind joined in this meeting of East and West: a meeting of biblical devotion and Hellenic civilization, of prophetic faith and philosophic thought. So it was that two divergent trends of spiritual life were unified. The divine message and the result of human endeavor, the word of God and the achievements of a nation most gifted and most creative in almost all fields of intellectual and artistic work touched one another. This was a memorable hour indeed, the hour of the birth of Western civilization with all its inner tensions and all its potentialities.

We can vividly imagine how the proud heirs of Athenian greatness and glory may have looked down upon the person who preached so strange a message—who dared to call their own religion superstitious—who had the bad taste to glorify a man put to a somber and dismal death on the cross—who was ignorant enough to believe in the resurrection of the flesh and insolent enough to exhort them to accept such a repellent faith.

Paul, however, was fully aware of the obstacles which confronted him. One has to admire the quiet superiority of his attitude. Without any fear he simply states his conviction. He is certain that his message holds a treasure which can conquer the philosophically well-trained and skeptical-minded Athenians. His very first words hit the weak spot of their spiritual situation: the chasm between their religious tradition and their philosophical erudition. He knows very well that this chasm has torn apart the city, and the soul of every citizen. He knows that their religion is no longer alive and that their living ideas, sublime and profound as they are, nevertheless cannot make good their lack of faith or become a new religion. He knows that these people, in spite of their seasoned civilization, are in spiritual distress and embarrassment. They know everything, but they believe in nothing. They criticize their own gods as their philosophers and poets have done for centuries; they even mock at them as Euripides and others have taught them to do. What is the good then of all their wonderful achievements? What is the good of their philosophical systems, if their life is devoid of real meaning, if the result of all their penetrating thought is spiritual doubt and despair?

In this context Paul mentions the inscription he has seen while strolling through the streets of the Greek city: "To the unknown God." Here the Greeks' whole spiritual plight comes to the fore. They do not know the living

God whom he is able to declare. The inscription is quite right: religiously they are ignorant in spite of their vast store of knowledge and wisdom. The living God whom Paul proclaims unites what is disunited in the Greek situation; he unites the religious life, which the gods once symbolized, with the sublimity and profundity of their philosophical ideas. Thus Paul offers them a cure for the spiritual sickness from which they suffer. He points to the empty place in their hearts, and shows them how this place can be filled.

Furthermore, Paul goes beyond this attempt. He turns directly to the philosophically schooled among his hearers in order to persuade them that the faith which he cherishes is the only true one; the faith in the living God, he argues, is in fact universal, even though God is hidden to most nations because of their superstitious imaginations. All nations are created by the same God. He has made them all of one blood, so that differences of race and birth cannot impede the recognition of the universal author of the universe. No human being is far from him. The universal God has impressed his own nature upon everyone. This argument was probably of great weight for those who believed in the realm of universals. Paul gave it an even stronger support by a phrase which has an almost pantheistic touch. God is near, he says, for in him we live and move and have our being. Continuing, he quotes the words of a Greek poet which he believes also point to the universality of the true God, the Maker of all and the Lord of all.

Paul can speak with so much poise and authority not

only because he is firmly rooted in his faith but also because he is both a son of the chosen people and a cosmopolitan, endowed both with biblical faith and Hellenic culture. The world in which he lives is ripe for the acceptance of a universal religion combining the message of Christ with speculative erudition. He comes into the harvest when the fruit of prophecy and the fruit of philosophy can be gathered together; when all the nations of the ancient ecumenical orb can join in the same spiritual community, when the fullness of time has arrived.

But as he approaches the end of his address, Paul does not spare the Athenians the abysmal paradox of his faith. Philosophic though this faith is, it is only so in part. Another element, and that element alone, makes Christianity a living faith as distinguished from all rational arguments. Paul's God is not only the universal supreme cause and substance of the world; he is also a loving Father of the one man, Jesus the Christ, who was sent to earth that all mankind might be saved. By pointing to Christ, Paul drops the diplomatic restraint and adaptation he has used at first to arouse the attention of his learned audience, and proceeds to challenge the philosophical bent of the Athenians. Philosophy, he seems to imply, is not religion. The living God is living precisely because he is more than the supreme cause and substance of the world, more than the ground of all being or the abstract idea of being as such: he is Lord and Father, Judge and Redeemer, and only thus is he the God of a living faith.

I cannot imagine that Paul was surprised when some

of his hearers scorned his message; he was perhaps more surprised that some wished to hear more about it.

Today we are in a spiritual situation not altogether different from that in which Paul preached to the Athenians. We too look back upon many centuries of a great and glorious cultural development, and many have arrived at the same point where they know everything (or at least think they do) but believe in nothing. Many feel the split between faith and culture and suffer from it. An immense and momentous contrast exists between the ancient situation and our modern plight. Although we too have our cynics and our boasting atheists, still the Ancient of Days is in our midst. We do not need a new Paul; we need only to remember Paul and to refresh his message in our minds and in our hearts.

XIX

A Deeper Beatitude

And we know that all things work together for good to them that love God, to them who are the called according to his purpose. For whom he did foreknow, he also did predestinate to be conformed to the image of his Son, that he might be the firstborn among many brethren. Moreover whom he did predestinate, them he also called: and whom he called, them he also justified: and whom he justified, them he also glorified. What shall we then say to these things? If God be for us, who can be against us? He that spared not his own Son, but delivered him up for us all, how shall he not with him also freely give us all things? Who shall lay any thing to the charge of God's elect? It is God that justifieth.

—Rom. 8:28-33

"All things work together for good to them that love God." In what sense is this assertion to be understood? Who are the people to whom all things work together for good? What things are working together that way and for what good? These questions are by no means easily answered, although the words of Paul are so familiar to us that everybody is ready to answer them in his own particular way. The first interpretation that comes to mind is probably the opinion so often uttered throughout the Bible, especially in the Old Testament, that the good are rewarded while the wicked are punished. The First Psalm eloquently expresses this belief in a moral order which unfailingly distributes good and evil according to merit.

> Blessed is the man that walketh not in the counsel of the ungodly . . .
> He shall be like a tree planted by the rivers of water, that bringeth forth his fruit in his season . . .
> Whatsoever he doeth shall prosper.
> The ungodly are not so: but are like the chaff which the wind driveth away . . .
> The Lord knoweth the way of the righteous: but the way of the ungodly shall perish.

The conviction that the innocent and just man deserves to be favored and is favored by God, and that the guilty one should and does suffer punishment, is so deeply rooted that such an interpretation of Paul's words seems both natural and morally suggestive. Indeed, if this fair balance

135

between character and destiny, between merit and blame, between good and bad luck does not exist, how can we uphold the belief in a just and powerful ruler of all things?

Life experience (even on a small scale) does not confirm this conception of a moral world order. It demonstrates, with abundant illustrations, that the neat equation of moral goodness and a bright fate does not stand the test. Certainly not all things work together for a happy life to those who love God. The suffering servant in Isaiah and the misfortunes of Job show that as early as Old Testament times there was an awareness that character and destiny disagree. It is simply not true that the godly man prospers and only the ungodly perishes. If this equation is made the measure for a moral world order, then the world in which we live is not morally ordered but to say the least is indifferent or impartial to the moral differences of persons. The Book of Job refutes and rejects the cheap explanation of Job's calamities as just punishment for the misdeeds of a troubled man. And Jesus bluntly pronounces this conviction erroneous: "[Our Father] maketh his sun to rise on the evil and on the good, and sendeth rain on the just and on the unjust" (Matt. 5:45). In ancient Greece, for the same reasons, Stoic philosophers abandoned the Platonic equation of happiness and virtue by teaching that man should retreat from the evident inequality inherent in human destiny and should find his peace and poise solely in the strength of his own inner independence. They recognized that not all things work together for good to them who love God.

Nothing demonstrates the fallacy of such a morally comfortable faith more strongly than the abysmal grief that befalls Jesus, the man of sorrows. The whole of the New Testament is one great refutation of the easygoing belief in a moral distribution of reward and punishment. The dismal outcome of the lovingkindness of the Lord is evidence enough that not all things work together for good to them who love God, that is if "good" means a gentle course of life, and if "all things" means the facts, circumstances, and conditions shaping the frame of fate. This verdict is corroborated by the words of Jesus spoken to his disciples: "In the world ye shall have tribulation" (John 16:33), and by these other words: "If any man will come after me, let him deny himself, and take up his cross daily" (Luke 9:23). The fate of those who dare to follow Christ is not mild and friendly, but harsh and bitter. All things do not work together for good to them, if "good" signifies pleasantness or agreeableness. Accordingly "good" also does not exempt them from conflicts and afflictions, from persecution and privation. Rather those who love Christ have to expect that all things will work together for a gloomy and tragic lot, because the world, governed by faction and strife, by ambition and arrogance, hates the lovers of peace and the men of good will. The world is not morally instituted, but is under the dominion of satanic powers.

What, then, does the solemn promise of Paul really mean? Has Paul fallen back to the more primitive belief of the Old Testament which equates moral goodness and the goodness of destiny? Is he simply mistaken?

There is only one solution to this riddle. Paul does not mean at all what his words seem to say when we interpret them in a narrowly moral or common-sense way. He means something infinitely more hidden and mystical. He does not point to moral goodness or to a happy destiny, not even to that inner independence which according to the Stoics grants inner peace and quiet of the soul. He does not imply that the outer circumstances and conditions of life will be favorable to the lovers of God and Christ, nor even that the inner strength of a man, his capacity of bearing hardship and enmity, will save him.

Paul gives us the clue to his words when he says: "He that spared not his own Son, but delivered him up for us all, how shall he not with him also freely give us all things?" "All things"—this is not all things that the world might give us, be it the outer or the inner world, nor gifts of the pagan deity, Fortune. What he really means is that deeper and hidden totality which is the ground of the whole world and of the human soul. It is God who is truly all things, because all things are generated by him. God will be on the side of those who love him. God, who is infinitely superior to all the facts and all the events which make up our destiny; God, who is infinitely superior to our own strength and capacities, will work for good. This good is not anything that can make us happy on earth, not even that highest kind of good which the ancients called wisdom and virtue, but it is the grace and love of God revealed in Christ; it is that peculiar fellowship with the Lord which bestows upon us a serenity and a beatitude deeper and more precious than anything that destiny or fate can give or take.

If we are allowed to enjoy the love of God, then nothing whatsoever can deprive us of that supreme good which alone is good in every respect and through all events, under all circumstances and under all conditions which nature or history may impose upon us. Then we are safe, even if we have to lose our life, yea even safest when we are called upon to give our life for him who gave it to us. "What shall we then say to these things? If God be for us, who can be against us?" All things work together for good to those who know that this promise is fulfilled on a level deeper than the alternative of fortune or misfortune, of success or frustration, of pleasure or pain—for who was more frustrated than Christ? Whose destiny was more painful? And yet in the midst of the greatest sorrow and the bitterest loneliness, Christ knew that it was God who made all things work together for good to those who love him.

XX

The Unfathomable Sublimity

O the depth of the riches both of the wisdom and knowledge of God! how unsearchable are his judgments, and his ways past finding out! For who hath known the mind of the Lord? or who hath been his counsellor?

—Rom. 11:33-34

The Bible abounds in sayings which stress the incomprehensibility of God. The Creator of the world and of man cannot be grasped by our finite understanding any more than he can be measured by our finite standards of judgment. He surpasses all searching, all thinking, all knowing. He knows me better than I can know myself. He dwells in a light which no man can ever hope to attain. He is too high, too great, too powerful, ever to be perceived or conceived. He is miraculous and wondrous, and we can approach him only in fear and trembling even when we love and adore him. He is everywhere, and therefore we cannot escape him; he is eternal and therefore in all times. How can we be so foolish as to believe that any theory or any philosophy will ever be able to break through this wall that surmounts all our capacities? How can we ever indulge in the illusion that any notion or category of our thinking mind can penetrate into the mystery of God?

The Bible teaches us God's transcendence on its every page, but the Bible does not lament or complain about our profound ignorance. On the contrary, the Bible regards the incomprehensibility of the Highest (the pledge and proof of God's transcendent glory and majesty) as the best safeguard against our pride and conceit. Only because God is beyond the reach of our knowledge can we adore and worship him. Only because he is hidden can we trust and love him. Only because we cannot measure him are we in his hands. We can praise but never rebuke him. We may wonder at his ways—we may even doubt whether he exists—but as long as we live within faith, we have no desire to understand his mind and to appraise his wisdom or justice. As long as we live in faith, we are overawed and fascinated by the unfathomable sublimity of him who created the heavens and the earth and who permits and even commands us to love him. The biblical believer does not begrudge splendor and might to God; on the contrary, he rejoices and exults at the very incomprehensibility of his Lord. He worships the mystery that shrouds God's existence.

He who commands the stars as he commands our wills is too great to be reached by reason or by reasons. He is too great even to be proved by argument. The very attempt to demonstrate the existence of the Creator only demonstrates the inability of man to feel the immeasurable depth of him who is beyond and above all measurement. If we tried to demonstrate his existence we would have to start from premises which controlled our conclusion. From no human premise could we possibly infer that he exists who is the source of all premises as well as of all conclusions, the Lord of life as well as the Lord of reason and of understanding, of all thinking and of all thought. The only adequate response of man facing the Supreme Being is to exclaim with the prophet: "Holy, holy, holy, is the Lord of hosts: the whole earth is full of his glory."

Does this mean that the Bible completely annuls and

prohibits all human thinking about the divine? Does it mean, in other words, that biblical faith excludes any philosophical theology? Certainly St. Paul warns against philosophy. But we may say that he only warns against a philosophy which is built as he says upon "vain deceit, after the tradition of men"; however, he adds "and not after Christ," thereby obviously denouncing all philosophy which does not rely upon faith. This radical verdict is in perfect agreement with the whole line of biblical wisdom. After all, the Bible begins with the story of man's sinful appetite for an unbounded knowledge which would exalt him to the rank of God himself. This appetite afflicts mankind with all the ills from which we suffer. If man tries to transgress against the proper boundaries of his created nature, be it by acts or by thoughts, God punishes him. Philosophy, aiming at the comprehension of God by ignoring man's true dimensions and by abandoning faith, is not only outrageous, but is also doomed to fail according to biblical standards. Whenever man tries to conquer the throne of the Highest with his own mind, he must necessarily be frustrated. The wisdom of man is foolishness in the sight of God, just as God's wisdom is foolishness in the sight of man. There is no common denominator between the ways of finite reason and those of the infinite Spirit.

The ultimate notion to which philosophy can attain is "being." When we think of being, we seem to embrace everything that is—the whole universe visible and invisible, we seem to transcend the horizon of all things merely

finite, particular, and temporal, we seem to attain the
zenith of all existence, the summit of all thought. Plato
had already seen that there is something beyond and above
being and beings, and this he called the Good in itself,
the Absolute Good. The Good as such, he said, "outshines
by far in dignity and power" everything else; it exceeds
even the whole of reality, the essences of all things. He
felt that the Good is in itself more mysterious and more
ultimate than anything we may think. If we dare to con-
ceive of God by human thoughts, we should follow Plato;
we should comprehend him as the Good personified. The
Bible reveals that the Supreme Being is more than a principle or notion. Even the Good taken as a principle can
not reach him. Only if the supreme Good is a supreme
person can we approach the living God, and this assump-
tion would agree with Plato's statement that the Good in
itself is the ultimate cause of all things, even of all our
knowledge and of all the truth we may attain. Only if
God is mysteriously akin to us can we be created in his
image; only if we are created in his image and if he is
akin to us, can we love and fear him, pray to him and
worship him as our Lord and Father. "Being" as such
cannot be our refuge and our shield, it cannot know our
thoughts, it cannot judge us, it cannot forgive us, it cannot accept us, it cannot redeem us.

God is Holy Will, incomprehensible yet commanding
our own wills, unfathomable yet loving the sinner, hidden yet revealing himself in his son Jesus Christ. Only
so is the Good more than an idea and more than being

as such. Only so is it God: Creator and King! "O Lord, thou hast searched me, and known me. Thou art acquainted with all my ways. Thou hast beset me behind and before, and laid thine hand upon me. Such knowledge is too wonderful for me; it is high, I cannot attain unto it."